THEOLOGY AND POETRY

THE LITTMAN LIBRARY OF
JEWISH CIVILIZATION

Dedicated to the memory of
LOUIS THOMAS SIDNEY LITTMAN
*who founded the Littman Library for the love of God
and as an act of charity in memory of his father*
JOSEPH AARON LITTMAN
and to the memory of
ROBERT JOSEPH LITTMAN
who continued what his father Louis had begun
יהא זכרם ברוך

*'Get wisdom, get understanding:
Forsake her not and she shall preserve thee'*
PROV. 4: 5

*The Littman Library of Jewish Civilization is a registered UK charity
Registered charity no.* 1000784

Theology and Poetry

◆

Studies in the Medieval *Piyyut*

◆

JAKOB J. PETUCHOWSKI

London
The Littman Library of Jewish Civilization
in association with Liverpool University Press

The Littman Library of Jewish Civilization
Registered office: 4th floor, 7–10 Chandos Street, London W1G 9DQ

in association with Liverpool University Press
4 Cambridge Street, Liverpool L69 7ZU, UK
www.liverpooluniversitypress.co.uk/littman

Managing Editor: Connie Webber

Distributed in North America by
Oxford University Press Inc., 198 Madison Avenue,
New York, NY 10016, USA

First published 1978 by Routledge & Kegan Paul Ltd for
The Littman Library of Jewish Civilization
First issued in paperback 2004

Catalogue records for this book are available from the
British Library and the Library of Congress

ISBN 978–1–904113–16–4

Printed and bound in Great Britain by
CPI Group (UK) Ltd., Croydon, CR0 4YY

Contents

In memory of my dear Mother,
who taught me the poetry of faith

Introduction and Acknowledgments

Theology, by definition, is the rational discourse about God, and, by extension, the rational discourse about religious matters in general. Man is a rational—though not *only* a rational—creature, and, as such, he is ever striving to verbalize, to rationalize, and to systematize. If God is the highest of which man can conceive, it follows that man not only tends to rationalize and systematize his conceptions of God, but also that he is prone to view his rational discourse about God as the highest form of rational discourse.

Thus it was that, for many centuries, theology could rule man's intellectual endeavors as the Queen of the Sciences. Only in more recent generations did the sciences rebel against their 'handmaiden' status and become queens in their own right— queens, moreover, who would not infrequently challenge the 'established conclusions' and absolute certainties of their erstwhile mistress, theology.

Theologians may have reacted to the demotion of their discipline with good or ill grace, but, by and large, they were in no doubt about the fact that theology was, at any rate, one of the sciences, even if she was no longer *prima inter pares*, let alone the 'queen' of all human intellectual enterprises. Admittedly, the philosophic garb in which theology appeared, and the metaphysical weapons with which she defended herself, changed from time to time—even as the various philosophical systems with which theology had periodically aligned herself were subject to

I

the changing intellectual fashions among men. There have been Platonic theologians and Aristotelian theologians, Neo-Platonic theologians and Idealistic theologians, just as, at the present time, we have Existentialist theologians as well as theologians who accept the limitations placed on them by Logical Positivism.

However, in all of those alliances, theologians have not seldom lost sight of the fact that theology is an interpretive discipline, rather than itself a primary source of religious knowledge. As Samuel S. Cohon has put it: 'Theology is to religion what grammar is to speech.'[1] Experience, says Cohon, must not be identified with its interpretation. 'Religion, supplying the data of theological investigation, naturally precedes theology, even as flowers precede botany, or as health precedes hygiene or medicine.'[2]

For a long time it had been the practice of theologians to offer rational proofs for the existence of God. Theologians have become more diffident about furnishing such proofs since Immanuel Kant, in his *Critique of Pure Reason* (1781), has demonstrated that such 'proofs' can be demolished with the same kind of logic with which they can be constructed. More recently, Karl Barth has insisted on identifying the attempt to prove the existence of God rationally with sheer idolatry. A God concept constructed by man's mind is, for Barth, no less idolatrous than gods of wood and stone fashioned by man's hands.

Perhaps Barth was unduly harsh in his condemnation of the attempt to prove God's existence rationally. After all, we can hardly conceive of the medieval theologian as sitting down with a blank mind and an uncommitted heart, laboriously arriving at a syllogistic conclusion to the effect that there must be a God. The medieval theologian—with all of his protestations of rationality— was far more likely to have been a fervent religious believer who sought to express his deepest convictions in the verbal coinage of the contemporary universe of rational discourse. Karl Barth would indeed allow as much to St Anselm of Canterbury.[3] But the same would seem to apply to other theologians besides St Anselm, and to other traditional proofs for the existence of God as well as to St Anselm's 'ontological proof.'

Yet if theology is rational discourse *about* a primary experience, rather than that experience itself, we are faced by the problem whether that rational discourse can really do full justice to the primary experience. What if that experience transcends the capacity of rational discourse? What if it involves aspects of the human personality which lie beneath the level of consciousness? What, finally, if, by its definition, the very subject matter of theology eludes the human grasp?

In that case, we would have to admit that, far from dealing with clearly definable data as the physical sciences do, or with the type of analytical mental constructs which form the subject matter of metaphysics, theology is compelled to rely on intimations. This was already expressed by the biblical writer who had Moses ask God, 'Oh, let me behold Your Presence!,' only to be told, 'You cannot see My face, for man may not see Me and live.' But God also said to Moses: 'See, there is a place near Me. Station yourself on the rock and, as My Presence passes by, I will put you in a cleft of the rock and shield you with My hand, until I have passed by. Then I will take My hand away and you will see My back; but My face cannot be seen.'[4]

When we speak of something *of* which we only have hints and intimations, we can speak of it likewise only *in* hints and intimations. We can allude to it, and we can suggest it; but we can hardly formulate it in propositions which will pass muster before the bar of logical rigor. We had, therefore, best express it in the images and the nuances of poetry.

It has actually been suggested by Walter Kaufmann that the theologian should regard himself as dealing with poetry, rather than with science and metaphysics.[5] Although Kaufmann holds that 'religion is poetry, but not "mere" poetry,'[6] and, as such, he is able to appreciate religion, his words are nevertheless those of a severe critic of the whole theological enterprise as it has thus far been conducted; and they have, therefore, had no perceptible impact upon the professional theologians. Yet, to suggest the link between theology and poetry does not necessarily always mean that the work of the theologian is not being appreciated.

Approaching the subject from quite a different perspective,

3

Henry Slonimsky has argued that 'whatever in philosophy is capable of translation or transformation into poetry is alone vital and valuable; and . . . whatever has originally been conceived as myth is alone real and effective, for it is something capable of being believed and therefore loved.'[7] It is interesting to note in this connection that Slonimsky was writing as a philosopher, rather than as a theologian—which, perhaps, makes his evaluation of myth and poetry even more striking.

There is no reason why the theologian, too, could not admit—while making no apologies for the fact that there are times and situations when rational discourse about God and religion is both wholesome and inescapable—that the data with which theology is working are data derived from a realm of poetry and myth. Nor is there any reason for him to deny that only those elements of his theological system which can be translated and transformed into poetry will retain their value and their vitality.

This, in fact, is what has always happened in Judaism. By the side of its technical theological tractates, Judaism has had its prayerbook—next to the Pentateuch, the Prophets and the Psalms, practically the only 'theological' *vade mecum* which many Jews, throughout the centuries, have had at their immediate disposal. And the language of prayer is, of necessity, the language of poetry. Theological systems may come and go; but the theology which is translatable into liturgy remains. Maimonides' need to square his Judaism with his Aristotelianism may be a need which, at any rate, in those specific terms, is no longer felt. But the poetic recasting of Maimonides' theological propositions is still a part of Jewish worship. The peculiar theology of the German Jewish Pietists of the twelfth and thirteenth centuries, with its near-Gnostic distinction between the Hidden God and the Glory of God accessible to man, is a theology shared by few, if any, modern Jews. But the Hymn of the Glory, to which that theology gave birth, continues to be sung in the synagogue.

If poetry is the medium through which 'normative' theology ('normative' at least for its time and place) best expresses itself, then poetry becomes a still more fitting medium for the expression of theological views which, even if they are not fully heretical,

4

nevertheless represent a challenge to what has become normative and conventional. We are, of course, not speaking of the kind of heresy which is a downright denial of fundamental religious principles, but of the kind of 'argument with God' which is one, though by no means the sole, posture typical of the Jew's relation to the Deity. We mean the challenges hurled at God—in prayer.

Statements and arguments which, in prose, would immediately be branded as 'heretical' have become, once they were couched in poetic form, ingredients of the liturgy, and continue to be rehearsed—often with more devotion than comprehension—by multitudes of the unsuspecting pious who would be utterly shocked to discover the true intent of their authors. It does happen, of course, that, on occasion, the gap between the poet's concern and the 'normative' theology of the moment becomes apparent; and then we find purists like Maimonides fulminating against 'the truly ignorant poets or such as think that what they speak is poetry,' and castigating those poets for composing 'vituperative utterances against what is above.'[8]

Yet, on the whole, the protests of Maimonides and those who thought like him have been of no avail. Liturgical poems expressing the unconventional and the idiosyncratic continued to share the same prayerbook pages with formulations of the generally accepted and conventional notions of Jewish theology. The conventional and the unconventional shared the same pages of the prayerbook as they had always shared the same pages of the Talmud and of the Midrash, where no uniformity of theological positions was ever enforced nor ecclesiastical control of religious feelings intended. Indeed, novel and startling as some of the ideas expressed by the medieval poets may have been in contrast to what, by the poets' time, had become crystallized as *the* 'normative' theology, few, if any, of those ideas were altogether without precedent within the vast reaches of Rabbinic literature.

That much had already been recognized by Abraham Ibn Ezra (1089–1164). Bible commentator, philosopher, and himself a composer of synagogal poetry, Ibn Ezra was one of the most severe critics ever to speak out against the kind of poetry which had entered the synagogue service by his time. He criticized that

5

poetry on aesthetic as well as on grammatical grounds. But he also noted, in his critique of Eleazar Kallir,[9] that

> all of his poems are full of exegetical and homiletical allusions, whereas our Sages had said that no biblical verse ever departs from its literal meaning. It is, therefore, proper to pray only in a literalist manner, and not in a manner containing mystery or parable, or in a manner not in consonance with the accepted legal rulings, or, again, in a manner which lends itself to a variety of different interpretations.

There may indeed have been moments in Jewish history when the poetry of Jewish liturgy was mistaken for prose. The nineteenth century was such a time, when traditionalists made dogmas out of prayers, and when modernists, insisting on the literal truth of every liturgical phrase they uttered, omitted large segments of the prayerbook because they were not, in any prosaic and literalist sense, 'true.'[10] But, apart from those isolated moments in a long history, Ibn Ezra's advice to 'pray only in a literalist manner' was hardly the advice by which Jews let themselves be guided. The poetry of the synagogue proves it.

What Ibn Ezra noted in the case of Kallir, namely the use made by the poets of materials culled from the Midrash and the *Aggadah*, holds true for most medieval synagogal poets—at any rate, for those of the Franco-German school, who consciously tried to imitate the Kallirian style. Those of the Spanish school, on the other hand, were far less given to such demonstrations of midrashic virtuosity, preferring, instead, to model themselves on the biblical style. Yet Ibn Ezra's observation suggested to us the procedure adopted in this book.

Before presenting a poem on a given topic and commenting upon it, we first discuss the topic itself with references to the appropriate Rabbinic utterances about it. In this way, the reader will be able to judge for himself how a particular poet exercised his poetic originality, and to what extent he was merely casting in poetic form the generally accepted views of his time.

In selecting the poems for presentation here, we were primarily guided by the desire to introduce the reader to poetic expressions of unconventional and daring theological ideas which have been incorporated into the standard liturgy. Occasionally, however, we have selected poems of a more 'orthodox' bent. This we have done either to provide a foil to set into sharper focus the work of a particularly innovative poet, or because the poem we have selected expressed in a felicitous and original manner certain theological positions on which there was practically no disagreement within the ranks of traditional Jewry.

Since, moreover, the major emphasis in our selection has been poetry as a medium of theology, we have been somewhat limited in our choice; and we have, on purpose, excluded many a fine poem of praise or adoration or contrition which would grace any anthology of medieval poetry devoted to poetry as such, rather than to the more specialized interest of the present volume. It may seem ironical in the light of the criterion we have just described that, for the sake of maintaining balance and proportion, we have also found it necessary to exclude from this volume lengthy poetic creations meant to expound complete metaphysical systems. We are thinking in particular of Solomon Ibn Gabirol's 'Royal Crown,' which, however, the interested reader can now study in Bernard Lewis's recent translation.[11] The theological and philosophical content of Ibn Gabirol's other poems has been systematically analyzed by Karl Dreyer;[12] and an altogether new perspective on that subject is forthcoming from the pen of Professor Frederick P. Bargebuhr.

A uniquely difficult problem was that of the English translation of the poems. Half a century ago, Anglo-Jewry was blessed with a whole galaxy of fine craftsmen (and, it should be noted, craftswomen) in the difficult art of rendering medieval Hebrew poetry into intelligible and pleasing English. Herbert M. Adler, Arthur Davis and Elsie Davis, Alice Lucas, Nina Salaman, and Israel Zangwill, all made the treasures of medieval Hebrew poetry accessible to the non-Hebraist; and, to the extent to which their translations are still included in prayerbooks on both sides of the Atlantic, many a Jewish worshipper to this day is indebted to them and to their work.

7

Still, when faced by the choice between translating a Hebrew poem literally, thereby preserving its subtle allusions and nuances while sacrificing its poetic grace, and re-creating the poem anew in English, sacrificing allusions and nuances on the altar of English rhyme and meter, the Anglo-Jewish school of translators opted for the latter. That still made it possible for their paraphrastic translations to be used devotionally, but it also rendered their work practically useless for the purposes of the present volume.

In three instances only—poems no. 1, no. 2, and no. 5—have we given in to the temptation of approximating in English the beat of the Hebrew original and of attempting some kind of English equivalent to the Hebrew rhyme scheme. We trust that we have succeeded in doing so without concealing and disfiguring any of the overtones and undertones of the Hebrew composition, and without too much 'padding' to achieve an English rhyme. For the rest, we have preferred to let the ideas of the poems speak fully for themselves, even though it often meant that the poetic quality had to give way to prosaic intelligibility.

Israel Abrahams once remarked that 'Chaucer's lament of the unsuitability of rhyme to English applies with tenfold force to Hebrew.'[13] Imagine, then, the almost impossible task of trying to capture a Hebrew rhyme scheme in an English translation. It is easy to see why Israel Zangwill and his colleagues preferred to write poetic paraphrases to literal translations which would also be poetical. But it should also be clear to the reader that, in view of the nature of the present work, such an option was not available to us. Friedrich Leopold von Stolberg, the German translator of Homer's *Iliad*, pleaded: 'O dear reader, learn Greek, and throw my translation into the fire.' *Mutatis mutandis*, we feel like echoing that plea.

On the subject of translations, it should be pointed out that all translations from the Hebrew which appear in the text of this book—be they sections of the prayerbook, stanzas of poems by Ibn Gabirol or Bialik, and the like—are our own. This applies even to those passages for which page references are given to readily available editions of the liturgy. We have, in each instance, given those references in order to enable the reader both to consult the Hebrew original and to familiarize himself with the liturgical context in which those passages appear.

In the case of the poems which are the main topic of this volume, we have referred the reader to the most accessible source as well as, where available, to the appropriate listing in Israel Davidson's *Thesaurus of Mediaeval Hebrew Poetry* (2nd ed., New York, 1970, 4 vols), where further information about the poems and their liturgical use may be found.

To turn from the general to the personal, I would like to remind the reader that *Theology and Poetry* is meant to be an informative work, not a partisan tract. I have tried to deal sympathetically with every poet and his theological position. I may personally feel that the one or the other of them has something to contribute to the solution of some of the theological problems facing the Jew in today's world. But it would be a mistake to assume that the inclusion of a given poet or poem in this volume is in any way indicative of my own theological position. As far as the latter is concerned, I have tried to explicate it elsewhere.[14] The present work is an exercise in *historical* theology.

Gratefully I acknowledge the permission granted by Behrman House, Inc., New York, to use, in chapters I and X, material which, in a somewhat different form, has been contributed by me to the volume *Literature of the Synagogue* by Joseph Heinemann with Jakob J. Petuchowski, New York, Behrman House, 1975.

Finally, it is my pleasant task to express my thanks to those who, in one way or another, have been of assistance to me by supplying relevant information for the writing of this book. They are Professors Aaron Mirsky and Ezra Fleischer of the Hebrew University, Jerusalem; my good friend, Dr Michael Brocke of the University of Regensburg; and my former student and now cherished colleague, Professor Lawrence A. Hoffman of the Hebrew Union College in New York. I am also very grateful to

9

my friend of more than thirty years' standing, L. T. S. Littman, Esq., of London, who extended the initial invitation which led to my undertaking this work.

Tu BiShevat 5735/27 *January* 1975

CHAPTER I

The Poetry of
the Synagogue

The traditional Jewish liturgy, as it has come down to us, consists not only of the standard prayers ordained in the Talmud and the ritual codes, but also contains poetic embellishments of all kinds. Such poetic embellishments take the form of hymns to be sung prior to, and after, the standard prayers, and of poetic inserts in the standard prayers themselves. Thus, for example, there are occasions when each of the first three benedictions of the Sabbath or Festival *'Amidah* is interrupted by one or more poems. The same can happen to the first two benedictions before the *Shema'*, and to the benediction after the *Shema'* in the morning service, or to the two benedictions after the *Shema'* in the evening service.[1]

Technically, such poetic embellishments and inserts are known as *piyyutim* (singular: *piyyut*), a word which comes from the same Greek root that gives us the English words 'poet' and 'poem.' Some of the *piyyutim* are mere elaborations on the themes of the standard prayers. If, for example, a prayer mentions the celestial choirs praising the Lord, a poem inserted into that prayer may go into detailed descriptions of how the angels are organized, how they are taking turns in singing, etc. But very often a *piyyut* will bring in extraneous matter. Thus, into the standard benedictions of the *'Amidah* it may introduce a poetic treatment of the Torah and Haphtarah readings of that particular day, elaborating on the legal (*halakhic*) and homiletical (*aggadic*) interpretations of the biblical texts.

The origins of the *piyyut* are still a matter of scholarly debate. For a long time, scholars have been particularly intrigued by two twelfth-century reports. One is by Judah ben Barzillai Al-Bargeloni, who makes the point that, originally, *piyyutim* had been introduced during times of persecution:[2]

> The enemies decreed that Israel must not occupy themselves with the Torah. Therefore the Sages among them ordained for them, in the midst of the prayers, to mention, and to warn the ignorant about, the rules of Tabernacles on Tabernacles, and the rules of the other festivals and the rules of the Sabbath and the minutiae of the commandments by way of praises and thanksgivings and rhymes and *piyyutim*.

Modern scholars have interpreted this passage as referring to the law of the Byzantine emperor Justinian, who in 553 CE ruled in favor of reading the Greek translation of the Scriptures in the synagogues, while, at the same time, prohibiting *deuterosis*—a word which is generally taken to mean the *aggadic* exegesis of the *midrashim*.[3]

Yet another twelfth-century report specifically locates the origin of the *piyyut* in the Persian realm. That report comes from Samau'al b. Yaḥya al-Magribi, a Jewish convert to Islam, whose father was himself a synagogal poet of note. Samau'al writes:[4]

> The Persians forbade them [i.e., the Jews] the practice of circumcision and likewise prayer, because they knew that most of the prayers of that community were invocations of God against the nations—that He destroy them and make the world desolate, except for their own fatherland which is the Land of Canaan. But when the Jews saw that the Persians were serious about the prohibition of the worship service, they composed [new] prayers into which they inserted passages of the customary prayer. They called those [new] prayers *al-ḥizana*. They composed for them many tunes. At times of prayer, they would congregate to sing and to read . . . The remarkable thing about this is that, when Islam permitted the *ahl al-dimma* ['tolerated people,' i.e., the Jews under Muslim rule] the practice of religion, and when the obligatory prayer was permitted to them again, the *ḥizanat* had become for the Jews a meritorious religious exercise on festivals and holy days. They made them a substitute for the obligatory prayer, and were satisfied with it without being forced to do so.

While Samau'al, whose report is altogether somewhat garbled, does not give us any specific date for the introduction of al-ḥizana (which is what *piyyutim* are called in the Arabic-speaking world), we do know that the period between 450 and 589 CE, the end of the Sassanian reign in Persia, was a period of persecution for the Jews. There may well be some substance to Samau'al's report, and the Jews of Persia may well have substituted the singing of poetry for other (prohibited) religious exercises.

However, it is now beyond any doubt that the geographical origin of the *piyyut* lies in Palestine. If, therefore, Samau'al's report is true, all it means is that the Persian Jews adopted a Palestinian practice.

For that reason, Al-Bargeloni's account, read in the light of Justinian's law, tends to gain authority, since Palestine in the sixth century was part of the Byzantine world. Nevertheless, Al-Bargeloni's report does not compel us to date the beginning of the *piyyut* in the sixth century, for, as one scholar has argued, 'what is meant is that the Sages, at that time, included in the service *piyyutim* which were already in existence.'[5]

The earliest known *payyetanim* (authors of *piyyutim*) are Yosé ben Yosé, Yannai, and Eleazar Kallir, in that order. (There are a number of anonymous *piyyutim* of even earlier date.) It is now generally conceded that all three were Palestinians (a) because their poetry is based on a Palestinian, not the Babylonian, lectionary of the Pentateuch; (b) because the fragments of the standard prayers contained in their poetry point to the Palestinian, and not the Babylonian, rite; and (c) because, in Babylonia, the introduction of the *piyyutim* was opposed by many Rabbis as a Palestinian import.

But if we know where these three poets lived, we do not know when. All dates remain tentative and approximate. Thus, one scholar dates Yosé ben Yosé in the sixth century;[6] a second puts him as early as the second to the third centuries;[7] while a third points again to the sixth century 'or even earlier.'[8] Yannai, who is known to have lived before Kallir, is said by one writer to have lived some time around the fourth century,[9] by another 'between the end of the fourth and the beginning of the sixth centuries.'[10] And as for Kallir, the view of recent scholarship may be summed up by saying that he must have lived before the Arab conquest of Palestine in 635.[11]

Yosé, Yannai, and Kallir are the first three poets whose names are known to us. They are not, however, the first to have embellished the standard prayers with poetic elaborations. As Aaron Mirsky has argued, we must look for the origins of the *piyyut* in the talmudic age.[12] Indeed, Mirsky has devoted a whole volume to demonstrating that the early *piyyutim* reflect both the thought patterns and the speech patterns of talmudic *halakhah* and *aggadah*.[13] Hayyim Schirmann goes even further than this. He holds that *piyyutim* must have existed already in the second century CE. He insists that in the oldest standard prayers there may be found an embryo of the kind of rhyme which, later on, was to become a characteristic feature of the *piyyut*.[14] Similarly, Salo W. Baron points out that 'for a long time, there was little to distinguish the new creations [i.e., the *piyyutim*] from other prayers.'[15]

As against this, a later dating of the *piyyutim* has been argued by Ezra Fleischer, who maintains that the *payyetanim* did not begin their work until after the majority of the standard prayers had already crystallized;[16] and that, according to Fleischer, would get us at the earliest to the fifth century.[17] Fleischer sees in the *piyyutim* not an embellishment of the standard prayers, but a substitute for them,[18] even a kind of rebellion against them.[19] (Only later editions of the liturgy, including both the standard prayers and the *piyyutim*, make the latter look like inserts into the former.) Consequently, we have to assume the existence of fixed standardized prayers before we can account for the existence of the *piyyutim*.

What we have to bear in mind here is that, until the ninth century, there was no such thing as a Jewish prayerbook. The content of certain prayers was fixed, and so was the sequence of the prayers as well as the concluding eulogies of the major benedictions. But when it came to the actual wording of the prayers, a great deal of leeway was given—and more so in Palestine than in Babylonia. Not only did the precise wording of the prayers differ from congregation to congregation—so that, even in later centuries, no two manuscripts of the Palestinian rite are exactly alike—but also the same prayer leader in the same congregation may have chosen different words on different occasions for one and the same prayer.[20]

A prayer leader who also happened to be poetically gifted may well have elaborated a prayer poetically—thereby laying the foundations of the later, more formalized *piyyut*. In that sense, the *piyyut* would indeed represent a rebellion against the *idea* of standardized fixed prayers, although we need not assume (as Fleischer does) the existence of an actual body of such fixed prayers against which the poets rebelled.

One thing is quite clear. It was the prayer leader, in public worship, and not the congregation itself, who introduced and recited the *piyyutim*.[21] This not only stands to reason on account of the non-existence of written prayer manuals. It is also evidenced by one of the names given to one particular form of the early *piyyut*. That name is *qerobhah*, and it denotes the poetic embellishment of the *'Amidah*. Now the name *qerobhah* is derived from the name by which, in talmudic times, the prayer leader in public worship was known, and it may be argued, on the basis of that nomenclature, that the institution of the *qerobhah* must necessarily go back to those early times when, in public worship, the prayer leader began his function with the recitation of the *'Amidah*, and not before.[22]

All of this suggests, therefore, that, at a time when prayer texts were not yet fixed, several versions of the same prayer vied for popular acceptance—some more simple, others more elaborate or more 'poetic.' As prayer texts then became more fixed and more 'traditional,' particularly in the Babylonian rite, the earlier freedom to create liturgically presented itself, and was often fought, as an *alternative* to fixed prayer, until a compromise solution was arrived at. Not that the early stirrings of liturgical poetry were in any way elaborate structures of rhyme and meter; on the contrary. But the later kind of 'technical' *piyyut*, which may well have come to full flower as late as the sixth century, would nevertheless have been unthinkable without that earlier and much more simple foundation.

In the eighth, ninth, and tenth centuries, we find the Babylonian Geonim taking various positions on the question of permissibility of the *piyyut*. A few of them, under Palestinian influence, championed the *piyyut*'s cause; but there were many who vehemently argued against its introduction in Babylonia. Some went so far as to declare it wrong for the Palestinians themselves.[23] What was at stake here was not only an issue of *halakhah*, but also the question of hegemony over Jewish life, for which both the Palestinian and the Babylonian authorities were struggling at that time.[24] The *piyyut* had come to Babylonia from Palestine, and this fact alone made the Babylonians reluctant to give up their own tradition of not having *piyyutim* in favor of the Palestinian practice.

Ultimately, however, a compromise was achieved. Once certain *halakhic* specifications were met, the *piyyutim* could be tolerated. This becomes evident from a responsum of the ninth-century Gaon Natronai:[25]

> As for those who say *piyyutim* in the first two benedictions of the *'Amidah*, and in all the prayers, and include in them the subject matter of the festival on every festival, as well as inserts on the Ninth of Abh and on Purim—if, in every single benediction, they also deal with the subject matter of that benediction, and then, on Rosh Hashanah and Yom Kippur, they add words of appeasement and prayers for forgiveness, they are permitted to do so. But the main thing is that, in every single benediction, they bring in the theme of its beginning and of its end. And if, in between, they recite words of *aggadah* and praises of God, that is all right.

The initial *halakhic* argument against the *piyyut* had been that the *piyyut* interrupts the flow of ideas in the traditional prayers and benedictions by introducing thoughts which had nothing to do with the themes of the prayers into which they were inserted. Natronai, in—what we may call—the '*halakhic* compromise,' is willing to set that argument aside as long as the *piyyut*, at its conclusion, provides a 'bridge' to the theme of the concluding eulogy of the traditional benediction. It was on this basis that the *piyyut* won its legitimacy in those communities—and they were to become the majority—which accepted the authority of the Babylonian scholars.

But two points ought to be borne in mind. First, the 'halakhic compromise' was not universally accepted; at all times and in all places there have been great scholars who continued to oppose the *piyyut*.[26] And second, it should be noted that the 'halakhic compromise' declared the *piyyut* to be permitted, not to be mandatory.

Thus, Rabh 'Amram Gaon, in the ninth century, declares that, if the prayer leader wants to insert a *qerobhah*, he may do so. But 'Amram goes on to say: 'This is not something fixed nor is it an obligation. Rather is it whatever the congregation desires—be it to add or to omit.'[27] And Rabh Saadya Gaon, in the tenth century, seeing that 'now the majority have accepted the custom of saying Atonement *piyyutim* also in the morning service,' feels encouraged to set down three of his own.[28]

Two centuries later, however, Maimonides finds in the recitation of the *piyyutim* 'the major cause for the lack of devotion and for the lightheartedness of the masses which impels them to talk during the prayer . . . In addition, the *piyyutim* are occasionally the words of poets who are not scholars.'[29] This last point Maimonides elaborates in his *Guide of the Perplexed*, where, as we have already noted, he castigates the 'truly ignorant' poets and preachers, 'or such as think that what they speak is poetry,' for composing prayers and sermons in which attributes are predicated of God that run counter to true belief, and which constitute 'vituperative utterances against what is above.'[30] A number of the *piyyutim* which we present in the following pages, with their very pronounced anthropomorphisms, will, given Maimonides' philosophical position, suggest to the reader what he had in mind.

A century later, the author of the *Book of the Pious* complains about a man who left the synagogue after the special poetic penitential prayers in the morning service, without waiting for the recitation of the regular liturgy. This man was giving primary importance to secondary matters.[31]

But such objections notwithstanding, the *piyyut*, having once gained entry into the synagogue, continued to flourish. The mere listing of the names of the *payyetanim* takes up twelve pages in the new *Encyclopaedia Judaica*.[32] On European soil, we find the *piyyut* first developing in southern Italy, in the second half of the ninth century. From there, it spread, in the tenth century, to central and northern Italy. Franco-German Jewry, at first under Italian-Jewish influence, produced its own great school of *payyetanim* in the tenth and eleventh centuries—many of them composing in the style of Kallir, with his manifold allusions to biblical and Rabbinic literature and his grammatical peculiarities. The Spanish *piyyut* began to flourish in the tenth century. It is quite different in style and content from the Franco-German variety. It is couched largely in biblical vocabulary, adheres to classical Hebrew grammar, and adopts, often from Arab sources, sophisticated schemes of meter and rhyme.

While the *piyyut* continued to enjoy popularity, and while the number of *piyyutim* recited by congregations increased with the invention of printing and the availability of the printed prayer-book, few, if any, great *piyyutim* were composed after the thirteenth century.

Only in the nineteenth century did the preponderance of *piyyutim* in the synagogue service (particularly on festivals) begin to wane. Reform Judaism, in its endeavor to shorten the services, removed most of the *piyyutim* from its prayerbooks. But since then the number of *piyyutim* has also been severely curtailed in several Orthodox and Conservative rituals. In part, this is due to the fact that, without a commentary, many of the *piyyutim*—especially those of the Kallir type which predominated in the German-Polish rite—have become completely unintelligible to the modern worshipper. In part, too, the didactic *piyyut* which arose to take the place of the earlier Rabbinic exposition, the *derashah* (or the *deuterosis* of Justinian's law), had become super-fluous once the *derashah*, in the form of the modern sermon, had found its way back into the synagogue.

On the other hand, many Reform and Liberal, as well as Conservative, rituals have welcomed to their pages some of the poetic creations of our own time—both in Hebrew and in the vernacular. In that way, the devotional impetus, which, in addition to the historical factors we have surveyed in this chapter, was originally responsible for the rise of the *piyyut*, has found its outlet down to the present day. That impetus is the desire to infuse routine with spontaneity, to supplement ancestral piety with one's own religious expression, and, in the words of the Psalmist, to 'sing unto the Lord a new song.'

CHAPTER II

'The Creed Should be Sung!'

The late Bishop James A. Pike, of the Protestant Episcopal Church in the United States of America, is reported to have said: 'The Creed should be sung, not recited!' Pike was a religious liberal who was unable, in any literalist sense, to believe in the historical creedal formulations of the Church. Nevertheless, in a non-literalist approach, he was able to appreciate the faith of the historic Church which lay behind those formulations. He could appreciate it, and he could identify with it. But he could only do so if the Creed made no claim to be a full and adequate description of theological truth. That is to say, for Pike, the Creed was poetry, not prose; and, therefore, the Creed should be sung, not recited.

It is very doubtful whether the late bishop was at all acquainted with the minor details in the development of the synagogal liturgy. If he had been, he might have found some interesting precedents for his recommendation.

Unlike the liturgy of the Christian Church, Jewish liturgy did not, until fairly recent centuries, contain special rubrics set aside for a Creed. Creedal affirmations were, however, contained within the Jewish liturgy from the very beginning—such as the *Shema'*, proclaiming the Unity of God, and the surrounding prayers devoted to the themes of Creation, Revelation, and Redemption, respectively.[1] But those affirmations, which, with the exception of the quoted biblical passages, tended to vary in their wording from community to community and from one period of history to another, are not really comparable to such landmarks of Christian dogmatics and liturgy as the Apostles' Creed or the Athanasian Creed.

When, however, in the fourteenth and fifteenth centuries, creedal formulations were written for synagogal use, the poetic version, meant for congregational singing, preceded the prose version by a century.[2] Both versions entered the official prayer-book in the second half of the sixteenth century. But, while the poetic version became part and parcel of communal worship,[3] the prose version[4] was relegated to the position of material for *optional* private meditation after the conclusion of the statutory daily morning service. Thus, the Creed in the synagogue is never recited, but always sung. And for every Jew who silently reads the prose version after the end of communal worship, there are thousands who sing the poetic version as part of their statutory services. Bishop Pike might have liked that.

Altogether, the role of dogmas and creeds in Judaism is some-what controversial.[5] One often hears it said that 'Judaism is the religion of deed, and Christianity is the religion of creed.' But that is only a half-truth. Christianity, too, expects its followers to engage in deeds of love, motivated by faith—quite apart from the vast body of Canon Law accumulated by the Roman Catholic Church. As for the deeds of Judaism, their very claim to a Scriptural basis presupposes at the very least the ancient Rabbis' tacit acceptance of the following creedal axioms: (1) There is a God; (2) God has revealed Himself to Israel; and (3) Scripture contains God's revelation. There is, therefore, deed as well as creed in Christianity, and creed as well as deed in Judaism.

Nevertheless, it would be true to say that, historically speaking, Christianity has devoted far more time and energy to very minute and precise creedal formulations, while Judaism has devoted far more time and energy to minute and precise defini-tions of the deeds, both moral and ritual, expected of the Jew. In fact, in the vast literature of the Talmud there seems to be only one single passage which, with a reasonable amount of clarity, indicates a preoccupation with dogma. It is the first paragraph of the tenth chapter of the Mishnah tractate *Sanhedrin*. There it is stated that 'all Israelites have a share in the World-to-Come.' That all-embracing promise of eternal bliss is, however, immediately restricted by the following exclusions from the Hereafter: (1) He who claims that the doctrine of Resurrection is not grounded in the Pentateuch; (2) He who denies the divine origin of the Torah; and (3) The Epicurean.

What the teachers of the Mishnah meant by an Epicurean, they did not further specify. It is unlikely that they were thinking of, or that they even knew, the complete philosophical system of Epicurus. Yet they might have known about one of its more prominent features. Epicurus did not deny the existence of the gods. He merely denied that the gods concerned themselves with the world of men. Now, an assertion to the effect that God is unconcerned about the world, that, in Rabbinic parlance, 'there is no justice, and there is no Judge,'[6] would have been regarded as rank heresy and as the equivalent of atheism by the Rabbis. Perhaps it was that which they had in mind when they excluded the Epicurean from eternal bliss.

But, whether this was so or not, the Gemara's discussion of this Mishnah passage shows that later generations were no longer quite sure about what the Mishnah had in mind. The word, *apiqoros* (Epicurean), was thought by the teachers of the Talmud to be related to a Hebrew root, having the sense of 'freeing oneself from the yoke of the Law,' or from the authority of, and respect for, the Rabbis.[7]

When, in the twelfth century, Moses Maimonides (1135–1204) wrote his commentary on the Mishnah, he obviously also had to deal with the beginning of the tenth chapter of *Sanhedrin*.[8] He thought that the word *apiqoros* was an Aramaic word, signifying disdain of, and contempt for, the Torah and its traditional explanation, and that it was applied *inter alia* to 'those who do not believe in the fundamental principles of the Torah.'

Having mentioned those 'fundamental principles of the Torah,' Maimonides proceeds to a description of what they are. He enumerates and describes thirteen such principles: (1) The existence of the Creator; (2) The Unity of God; (3) The incorporeality of God; (4) God's absolute priority: no existent thing outside Him is primary in relation to Him; (5) God's exclusive claim to man's worship: the rejection of all mediators and idolatry; (6) Prophecy; (7) The superiority of the prophecy of Moses; (8) The divine origin and perfection of the Torah now in our hands; (9) The non-abrogation of the Torah of Moses: no other law will ever be substituted for it by God; (10) God's omniscience; (11) Divine Retribution: God rewards those who obey, and punishes those who transgress the laws of the Torah; (12) The coming of the Messiah; (13) The resurrection of the dead.

Maimonides' list of the fundamental principles of Judaism was not universally accepted either in his time or in succeeding generations. For one thing, Judaism in the twelfth century did not possess a supreme ecclesiastical body which, in a way comparable to Christianity, was in a position to promulgate dogmas. For another, the thirteen fundamental principles chosen by Maimonides had something arbitrary about them. Some thought that there were more than just thirteen fundamental principles; others felt that there were fewer. And, if there are to be thirteen, why just those particular thirteen?

This last question can be answered with relative ease. Many, though not all, of Maimonides' principles can best be understood in terms of a Jewish self-definition *vis à vis* the competing claims of both Christianity and Islam. As against the former, Maimonides maintained the absolute Unity of God, His incorporeality, His exclusive claim to man's worship which permits of no intermediaries, and the belief that the Messiah is yet to come. As against Islam, which was based on the assumption of some kind of 'progressive revelation,' Maimonides maintained the superiority of the prophecy of Moses over that of all of his successors, the perfection—and, therefore, the unchangeability—of the Torah of Moses, and the belief that God will not substitute another law for it.

Somewhat more complicated is the question why Maimonides saw fit to produce a compendium of the fundamental principles of Judaism in the first place. It has been suggested, and rightly so, we believe, that Maimonides understood the Mishnah's promise of a share in the World-to-Come for all Jews in terms of the concept of spiritual immortality as taught by medieval Aristotelianism. But, according to the latter teaching, immortality is possible only for those whose intellect is participating in the requisite metaphysical truths. Consequently, true immortality can be achieved, as it were, by philosophers and intellectuals only. Yet, with the exceptions already noted, the Mishnah promises immortality to *all* Jews—even to those who are not philosophers. What Maimonides, therefore, did was to provide, in capsule form, 'the minimum of knowledge which even the Jew without philosophical training must attain to participate in the truth of Judaism.'[9]

Maimonides was not the only medieval thinker who attempted to distil the essence of Judaism in the form of fundamental principles of the faith. Nor was Maimonides particularly popular with the upholders of 'orthodox' thought either during his life or after his death. And, as we have already seen, there was no ecclesiastical machinery which could have authoritatively promulgated Maimonides' principles as dogmas. All the more remarkable, therefore, is the fact that, within recent centuries, the principles enumerated and spelled out by Maimonides have become nothing less than the very yardstick by which modern Jewish 'orthodoxy' tries to define itself *vis à vis* the 'dissenting' views. So much so, indeed, that, in the early sixties of this century, a well-known Jewish scholar found himself barred from the principalship of Jews' College, England's seminary for the training of Orthodox Jewish clergy, for the sole reason that, in a book he wrote, he had expressed his acceptance of the methods of modern biblical criticism. That, however, was seen as a breach of the eighth principle of Maimonides, which declares that 'the Torah now in our hands' is identical with the one which Moses received at Sinai.[10]

Two factors are responsible, we believe, for the fact that it was the principles enumerated by Maimonides, and not those suggested by other medieval thinkers, which are recognized as dogmas by large segments of twentieth-century Jewry. One is the towering figure of Maimonides himself, and the moral authority he exercised—and still exercises—in the Jewish world. The other is the popularity of the poetic version of Maimonides' principles which has found its way into all synagogues.

Actually, the fourteenth century saw the composition of many different poetic versions of those principles, but only one of them, the *Yigdal* (poem no. 1), became incorporated into the liturgy.[11] The poem is now generally attributed to Daniel ben Judah, who lived in Italy around the year 1300, although, from time to time, other poets have been credited with its authorship.[12]

The popularity of *Yigdal* is so great that the poem has even been retained in the prayerbooks of Reform and Liberal Judaism which, by and large, however, tend to change the wording of the twelfth and thirteenth stanzas—to express the belief in a messianic age, rather than in a personal Messiah, and in spiritual immortality, rather than in physical resurrection. One of them has also found it necessary to indicate in a footnote to the ninth stanza that ' "His law" is here taken in a larger sense than it has in the original,' and to omit the seventh, eighth, and twelfth stanzas altogether.[13] But such radical tampering with the text of *Yigdal* has been rare in the history of Reform Jewish liturgy.

The appeal of *Yigdal* was felt beyond the confines of the synagogue. Thomas Oliver, a Wesleyan minister in the eighteenth century, heard the poem sung in a London synagogue, and was so impressed that he at once proceeded to translate it into English for use in churches—or, as he is reported to have put it himself: 'I have rendered it from the Hebrew, giving it as far as I could a Christian character.'[14] Oliver's version, entitled 'The God of Abraham Praise,' was published in 1772, and by 1799 it had reached its thirtieth edition. To this day it is still being sung in Anglican and other Protestant churches in the English-speaking world.

An adaptation of *Yigdal* by a Unitarian minister, Newton Mann, has found its way into the synagogues of American Reform Judaism. Entitled 'Praise to the Living God,' it is Hymn no. 54 in the third edition (1948) of the *Union Hymnal* published by the Central Conference of American Rabbis. Mann's adaptation ranges rather far afield from the original *Yigdal* and from

Maimonides' quite precise formulation. Thus, instead of affirming the Maimonidean doctrines of Revelation and the supremacy of Moses, Mann's hymn reads: 'His spirit floweth free, High surging where it will, In prophet's word He spake of old—He speaketh still.' And Maimonides' insistence upon the unchangeable character of the Mosaic Law turns in Mann's adaptation into: 'Establish'd is His law, And changeless it shall stand, Deep writ upon the human heart, On sea, on land.'

Beginning, then, with a somewhat ambiguous word in the third-century Mishnah, and Maimonides' twelfth-century commentary, explaining that word, followed by a fourteenth-century poet's versification of Maimonides' commentary, the synagogue acquired its Creed—a Creed meant to be sung. The fact that both Orthodox and Liberal Jews tended to adopt a literalist—not to say, pedestrian—approach to the wording of the Creed, leading the former to occasional heresy-hunts, and the latter to alterations of the text, would seem to belie the late Bishop Pike's assumption that a sung, rather than a recited, Creed can be appreciated on the level of poetry.

Still, the further fact that Christians could find inspiration in the *Yigdal*, and that the radical wing of Reform Judaism opened its hymnal to a Unitarian minister's adaptation of this poem, nevertheless underlines the observation that a Creed which is sung can be sure of a broader appeal than a Creed which is merely recited.

יִגְדַּל אֱלֹהִים חַי

מיוחס לר׳ דניאל בן יהודה

1 יִגְדַּל אֱלֹהִים חַי וְיִשְׁתַּבַּח
נִמְצָא וְאֵין עֵת אֶל מְצִיאוּתוֹ :

2 אֶחָד וְאֵין יָחִיד כְּיִחוּדוֹ
נֶעְלָם וְגַם אֵין סוֹף לְאַחְדּוּתוֹ :

3   אֵין לוֹ דְּמוּת הַגּוּף וְאֵינוֹ גוּף
לֹא נַעֲרוֹךְ אֵלָיו קְדֻשָּׁתוֹ:

4   קַדְמוֹן לְכָל־דָּבָר אֲשֶׁר נִבְרָא
רִאשׁוֹן וְאֵין רֵאשִׁית לְרֵאשִׁיתוֹ:

5   הִנּוֹ אֲדוֹן עוֹלָם וְכָל־נוֹצָר
יוֹרֶה גְדֻלָּתוֹ וּמַלְכוּתוֹ:

6   שֶׁפַע נְבוּאָתוֹ נְתָנוֹ אֶל
אַנְשֵׁי סְגֻלָּתוֹ וְתִפְאַרְתּוֹ:

7   לֹא קָם בְּיִשְׂרָאֵל כְּמֹשֶׁה עוֹד
נָבִיא וּמַבִּיט אֶת־תְּמוּנָתוֹ:

8   תּוֹרַת אֱמֶת נָתַן לְעַמּוֹ אֵל
עַל־יַד נְבִיאוֹ נֶאֱמַן בֵּיתוֹ:

9   לֹא יַחֲלִיף הָאֵל וְלֹא יָמִיר
דָּתוֹ לְעוֹלָמִים לְזוּלָתוֹ:

10   צוֹפֶה וְיוֹדֵעַ סְתָרֵינוּ
מַבִּיט לְסוֹף דָּבָר בְּקַדְמָתוֹ:

11   גּוֹמֵל לְאִישׁ חֶסֶד כְּמִפְעָלוֹ
נוֹתֵן לְרָשָׁע רָע כְּרִשְׁעָתוֹ:

12   יִשְׁלַח לְקֵץ יָמִין מְשִׁיחֵנוּ
לִפְדּוֹת מְחַכֵּי קֵץ יְשׁוּעָתוֹ:

13   מֵתִים יְחַיֶּה אֵל בְּרֹב חַסְדּוֹ
בָּרוּךְ עֲדֵי עַד שֵׁם תְּהִלָּתוֹ:

1 'GREAT IS THE LIVING GOD'
attributed to Daniel ben Judah

1 Great is the living God, and to be praised is He.
   He is; and His existence is of eternity.

2 One is He and unique, incomparable He;
   Unseen, and without end His unique Unity.

3 No human form has He, and He is bodiless;
   Nought is there to compare with His own holiness.

4 Before all things were made, the very First was He;
   And nothing came before His timeless primacy.

5 Eternal Lord is He; all things He did create
   His greatness and His rule declare and demonstrate.

6 His prophecy's outflow He richly has supplied
   To men of His own choice in whom He's glorified.

7 No prophet like Moshé in Israel did rise,
   Who looked upon God's likeness with his human eyes.

8 By hand of His Prophet, as faithful as can be,
   God gave unto His folk the Law of Verity.

9 God will not change His Law nor yet will He assay
   For it a substitute for ever and for aye.

10 All-seeing, He knows well the secrets now concealed;
   All outcomes from the first, to Him they are revealed.

11 The righteous He rewards, for his good deeds, with gain;
   He gives to wicked man, as he deserves, the pain.

12 And at the end of time Messiah He will send
   To save those who await salvation's promised End.

13 The dead He will revive in His abundant love.
   Bless'd through eternity His glorious Name above!

Commentary

The text of this poem may be found in *The Authorised Daily Prayer Book*, ed. Simeon Singer, 15th ed., London, 1935, pp. 2–3.

Its listing in Davidson's *Thesaurus* is in vol. 2, pp. 266ff., no. 195, where there is also a brief discussion about the identity of the poem's author, and where, in the face of hypotheses to the contrary, Davidson maintains that Daniel ben Judah, who lived in Italy around the year 1300, wrote this poem. See also Leopold Zunz, *Literaturgeschichte der synagogalen Poesie*, Berlin, 1865, p. 507.

The Hebrew original achieves its rhyme by having every stanza conclude with the possessive suffix of the third person masculine, attached to a feminine noun.

The Spanish and Portuguese rite and various Oriental rites add a fourteenth stanza, which reads: 'These are the thirteen principles; they are the foundation of God's law and of His Torah.' See *The Book of Prayer and Order of Service according to the Custom of the Spanish and Portuguese Jews*, ed. Moses Gaster, vol. 1, London, 1949, p. 91. But this stanza is evidently a later addition, and does not fit the meter of the previous thirteen stanzas.

1 *Great is the living God.* The usual translations, printed in various prayerbooks, have 'magnified be,' which is probably due to the fact that the word *weyishtabbah* ('and He is to be praised') also occurs in this stanza, and thus recalls the wording of the *Kaddish* prayer (*Authorised Daily Prayer Book*, pp. 77ff.) which does indeed begin with 'magnified be.' But the 'magnified be' of the *Kaddish* is *yithgaddal*, whereas our poem has the word *yigdal*—the identical word which occurs in Malachi 1:5, and which there must be translated as 'Great is the Lord beyond the borders of Israel.'

5 *all things He did create His greatness and His rule declare and demonstrate.* The standard versions have something like: 'He declares His greatness and His rule *to* every creature,' based on the Hebrew reading, *lekhol notzar*. That, however, is not at all the point of Maimonides' fifth principle which, rather, enunciates the creatures' duty to worship God alone. We have, therefore, adopted the reading *wekhol*, instead of *lekhol*, a reading attested to by David Nasi (fifteenth century) in his *Hoda-ath Ba'al Din* (Frankfurt aM, 1866), p. 10, and by an old printed Venetian edition of the prayerbook which was seen by S. D. Luzzatto. See *'Iyyun Tephillah*, in *Otzar Hatephilloth* (Vilna, 1914), vol. 1,

p. 55a. It is also the reading adopted by Philip Birnbaum in his edition of the *Daily Prayer Book* (New York, 1949), pp. 11–12. Birnbaum points out that the word *yoreh*, which we have translated in its double meaning of 'declare and demonstrate,' is used in b. *'Erubhin* 65a as an equivalent of 'pray.' See also Jakob J. Petuchowski, *Prayerbook Reform in Europe*, New York, 1968, p. 177.

7 *No prophet like Moshé in Israel did rise.* A direct quotation from Deuteronomy 34:10, but the sequence of the biblical words has been slightly rearranged.

Who looked upon God's likeness. Cf. Numbers 12:8 (about Moses): 'and he beholds the similitude of the Lord.'

8 *as faithful as can be.* Literally: 'the faithful one of His house.' Cf. Numbers 12:7: 'My servant Moses is not so; he is trusted in all My house.'

12 *salvation's promised End.* Literally: 'the end of His salvation,' where, however, 'end' does not mean the chronological termination of the act of salvation, but the act of salvation itself, i.e., the End of the normal course of history. For this eschatological meaning of the word 'end,' see Daniel 11:35; 12:4, 6, 9, and elsewhere in the Book of Daniel.

CHAPTER III

Speaking of God

Few problems have been as perennial for both the believer in, and the critic of, religion as the linguistic problem involved in speaking to and of God. Not only is this problem of great concern to the modern philosopher of religion,[1] but it was already recognized in the Bible itself, when Ecclesiastes (5:1) warned: 'Keep your mouth from being rash, and let not your heart be hasty to bring forth speech before God. For God is in heaven, and you are on earth; therefore let your words be few.'

If God is conceived as transcendent, that is, greater than the world and other than man, and if, in the nature of the case, man is limited to human speech, then speaking of God involves us in a twofold problem. On the one hand, if human language and discourse be burdened with the task of expressing something which, by definition, is ineffable and cannot be expressed, then the guardian of language and rational discourse may well conclude that the religionist is talking nonsense. This conclusion has, in fact, been reached by a number of modern linguistic philosophers—those approaching religion sympathetically insisting that they mean 'non-sense,' and not, pejoratively, 'nonsense.' On the other hand, from the religious believer's point of view, the application of mere human descriptive terms to the Deity borders, in its sheer inadequacy, on the blasphemous.

Thus, with some grammatical plausibility but doing violence to the context, a Rabbi in the Talmud can take the words of

Psalm 65:2, *lekha dumiyah tehillah* (commonly rendered as 'Praise befits You'), and understand them in the sense of 'For You, silence is praise.'[2] And, approaching the problem from a totally different angle, the modern linguistic philosopher, Ludwig Wittgenstein, warns: 'Of what cannot be said, thereof one must be silent.'[3] Maimonides, in the twelfth century, endeavors to work out a 'negative theology,' one which would confine itself to saying what God is *not*, rather than what God really *is*. And the twentieth-century psychoanalyst and thinker, Erich Fromm, insists that, 'while it is not possible for man to make valid statements about the positive, about God, it is possible to make such statements about the negative, about idols.'[4]

All such conclusions and advice may be both philosophically and religiously sound. However, the fact remains that most people do feel constrained at times to speak to and of God; and, when they speak, they speak in human language—with all of its inadequacies. They do, of course, differ in the degree of their recognition of those inadequacies.

The Bible itself, in spite of the *caveat* voiced by Ecclesiastes, to which we have already referred, purports to tell us a great deal about God; and, in so doing, it, of necessity, uses the language of man. Man understands no other. This was already realized by the second-century Rabbi Ishmael, who taught: 'The Torah speaks in the language of men.'[5] But the Bible does more than speak in human language. It also does not shy away from investing God with human organs—such as a hand or an arm—and human emotions, such as love and anger.

How much of this was meant by the biblical writers to be taken literally, and how much of it was a conscious metaphorical use of language, is still a matter of scholarly debate. It stands to reason that, when the Bible tells us that God delivered Israel from Egypt 'with a strong hand and an outstretched arm' (Deuteronomy 26:8), we are not meant to infer that God possesses human organs. But what are we to make of 'the Lord God walking in the garden toward the cool of the day' in Genesis 3:8? There can be no doubt that, still within the biblical period itself, that verse was already understood in a metaphorical sense, if not already in the sense of the later Midrash which connected the word 'walking' with 'the voice of the Lord God,' rather than with the Lord God Himself.[6] We may even grant that the editor who incorporated this verse—and the story in which it figures—into the Pentateuch understood it in a figurative, rather than in a literal, sense. But that still leaves unanswered the question about what was in the mind of him who originally told that story.

What we are dealing with is the problem of anthropomorphism, the representation of God under a human form or with human attributes and affections. Actually, there are two problems involved here. One is the theological justification, if any, for using anthropomorphic language in connection with God. That was one of the chief concerns of the medieval Jewish philosophers. The other has to do with the awareness of the problem itself on the part of the biblical and Rabbinic writers. It should be borne in mind, in this connection, that the Rabbis not only inherited the biblical anthropomorphisms, but that they also added many of their own. When, for example, the Song of Songs, in their interpretation, celebrates God's love for Israel, then all the descriptions of the young lover in that Song *ipso facto* become descriptions and attributes of God Himself.

Whatever modern scholarship may have to say about the literalist or metaphorical intentions of a given biblical writer, and whatever we may conclude about the biblical writers' awareness or lack of awareness of the 'problem' of anthropomorphism, it seems to be quite certain that the 'problem'—as seen by medieval philosophers and modern students—simply did not bother biblical man. Otherwise, we would find at least some indications of reflection and reluctance about this in the biblical text.

As far as the Rabbis are concerned, the question about their awareness of the 'problem' is far more complicated. We have already noted Rabbi Ishmael's recognition of the fact that 'the Torah speaks in the language of men.' Furthermore, many an utterance which strikes the modern reader as highly anthropomorphic is introduced, in the Rabbinic texts, by the word *kibheyakhol*, which means something like 'if one could possibly

33

say so.'[7] Moreover, in the *Targum*, the Aramaic paraphrase of the Scriptures, biblical statements to the effect that God did something or other are often, but not always, paraphrased to read that it was the *memra*, the Word of God, rather than God Himself, which engaged in that particular activity.

Yet the Rabbis were not unanimous in matters theological. They are, in fact, famous for the diversity of views which prevailed in their circles. It would, therefore, be futile to saddle *the* Rabbis with one particular attitude towards the problem of anthropomorphism, either for or against. That is why Arthur Marmorstein endeavored to show that there were actually two schools of thought among the Rabbis on the matter of anthropomorphism—one embarrassed by biblical passages of an anthropomorphic character, and, therefore, inclined to interpret them as metaphors, and one not so embarrassed, and, therefore, given to a more literalist interpretation. Marmorstein attributes the former position to Rabbi Ishmael and his disciples, and the latter position to Rabbi Akiba and his disciples. Akiba did not share Ishmael's axiom that the Torah speaks in the language of men.[8] Marmorstein's method and conclusions have, more recently, been followed by Abraham Joshua Heschel.[9]

But objections have been raised against the Marmorstein–Heschel approach as well as against the generally prevailing view that the *Targum* uses the figure of the 'Word of God' as a device to soften the anthropomorphism of biblical passages. As long ago as 1912, Joshua Abelson had argued that 'the view commonly taken that the *memra* is an expedient for avoiding the ascription of anthropomorphisms to the Deity, is only half the truth. As a matter of fact, the *Targum* is guilty of many anthropomorphisms.'[10]

Max Kadushin goes even much further than this. Arguing that the Rabbis and the philosophers simply do not inhabit the same universe of discourse, he insists that, for the Rabbis, the very problem of anthropomorphism did not exist. Value-concepts like God's love and His justice are, in any case, anthropomorphic or anthropopathic even as abstract concepts. Ascribing to the Rabbis any sort of stand on anthropomorphism is, according to Kadushin, a distortion of Rabbinic thought. 'When we employ the terms of classical philosophy even in an attempt to clarify rabbinic ideas, we are no longer within the rabbinic universe of discourse. Rabbinic statements about God arise as a result of interests entirely different from those of philosophic thought, represent human experiences that have nothing to do with speculative ideas.'[11]

It is difficult not to agree with Kadushin about the different origins of Rabbinic statements about God, on the one hand, and of philosophic thought and speculative ideas, on the other. Still, one can also not rule out the likelihood that, here and there, some—though not all—Rabbis may have been confronted by the necessity of examining their religious heritage and personal beliefs from the vantage-point of speculative ideas. Such a necessity would certainly have arisen in the face of doctrinal challenges the occurrence of which, by the Rabbis' own testimony, was not altogether rare in their time. It is, moreover, difficult to see how the Rabbis could have avoided an awareness of the anthropomorphic problem in their dealing with the exegetical claims of prevalent Gnosticism and rising Christianity.

Be that as it may. On the whole, Kadushin's argument, that the problem of anthropomorphism belongs to the realm of philosophical speculation rather than to the daily religious pre-occupations of the Rabbis, would seem to be valid. It is for this reason that the problem of anthropomorphism has loomed large whenever there has been a direct confrontation between the religious tradition of Israel and the philosophical tradition of Hellas. This was so in the large Greek-speaking Jewish community of Alexandria in Egypt; and we find the anthropomorphisms emphatically rejected and overcome through allegory by Philo of Alexandria (*ca.* 20 BCE–*ca.* 50 CE).[12] And that was so again when, after the rise of Islam, the Greek philosophical writings, in Arabic translation, became accessible to the Arabic-speaking Jews of the Mediterranean world. Here, the most outstanding Jewish thinker was, of course, Moses Maimonides (1135–1204), whose preoccupation with, and rejection of, anthropomorphism was, without doubt, the most thorough-going of all. Indeed, in his introduction to the *Guide of the*

Perplexed, his philosophical *magnum opus,* Maimonides states explicitly:[13]

> The first purpose of this treatise is to explain the meanings of certain terms occurring in the books of prophecy. Some of these terms are equivocal; hence the ignorant attribute to them only one or some of the meanings in which the term in question is used. Others are derivative terms; hence they attribute to them only the original meaning from which the other meaning is derived. Others are amphibolous terms, so that at times they are believed to be univocal and at other times equivocal . . . This treatise also has a second purpose: namely, the explanation of very obscure parables occurring in the books of the prophets, but not explicitly identified there as such.

The various terms and parables which Maimonides set out to explain are those fraught with anthropomorphism.

Maimonides had his predecessors, both Muslim and Jewish. First among the latter was Saadya Gaon (882–942), who may be considered to have initiated the systematic presentation of Jewish theology in the middle ages. Saadya devoted the second chapter of his *Book of Doctrines and Beliefs* to an exposition of the Unity of God. Stressing the absolute incorporeality of God, Saadya described the anthropomorphisms of the Bible as metaphors which must not be understood literally. As for the 'visions of God' reported by the biblical Prophets, Saadya argued that the Prophets did not see God Himself, but only the 'Glory' of God, which was itself *created* by God. This 'created Glory' (*kabhod nibhra*) Saadya identified with the *Shekhinah* (God's Presence) in Rabbinic literature. For Saadya, the sole function of that 'created Glory' was in revelation. It was not connected with the creation or the governance of the world.[14]

While, in his *Book of Doctrines and Beliefs,* Saadya made a distinction, in principle, between the 'created Glory' and the 'created Word,' he had combined the two into one inseparable whole in his earlier commentary on the mystical *Book of Creation* (*Sepher Yetzirah*).[15] Both that commentary and a paraphrase of the chapter on the Unity of God were to find their way to the Jews of Germany, where, in the twelfth and thirteenth centuries, a mystical and pietistic movement came into being, known as the *Hasidé Ashkenaz,* i.e., the German Pietists.[16]

The German Pietists represented a rather unusual mixture of mysticism and rationalism. On the one hand, in their devotional life, their stress on the number of letters in the statutory prayers from which they allowed no deviation almost bordered on the magical.[17] On the other hand, their fight against assigning any corporeal attributes to the Deity paralleled that of Maimonides himself.[18] And yet, their speculative and liturgical creations are the repository of an abundance of anthropomorphisms!

This was accomplished by the use which the German Pietists made of the Saadya materials which circulated among them, as well as on the basis of some other philosophical influences.[19] They distinguished between the 'Hidden God,' to whom they referred as the 'Creator,' and of whom they denied all corporeal attributes, and the 'Revealing God,' whom they identified with Saadya's 'created Glory,' and about whom they considered it legitimate to speak in anthropomorphic terms.[20]

While, therefore, the Hidden God was, by definition, un-knowable, and His existence could not be inferred even from the order of nature (but only from the super-natural miracles through which He manifested Himself),[21] the intense devotional life of the German Pietists concentrated on the 'Glory.' Indeed, they created what has been called a 'Glory theology.'

It is from the circles of the German Pietists that poem no. 2 has come down to us. The unabashed anthropomorphisms in which this poem wallows, and which have usually been toned down somewhat by previous translators into English, may shock the religious susceptibilities of the modern reader. What has to be borne in mind, however, is the fact that the German Pietists were obviously not addressing their hymn to a philosophical 'God concept,' such a concept being quite beyond anthropomorphic description even in their theological system, but to the God of religious experience, i.e., the 'Glory.' Here was the realization that, if one were to speak to and of God at all, one could not avoid the use of human language; and, once one had settled for the use of human language, it stood to reason that the more intense the religious experience, the more concrete that language tended to be.

Henry Slonimsky has reminded us that 'anthropomorphisms
are the device of our intelligence to say mythologically what we
are afraid or unable to say in bald abstract prose.'[22] Perhaps that
is the reason why, in spite of the ultimate disappearance of the
peculiar 'Glory theology,' with its Gnostic overtones, from the
religious consciousness of the Jew, the Hymn of the Glory has
maintained its honored place (sung as it is while the Holy Ark
is open) in the liturgy of the Ashkenazi rite to this day.

שיר הכבוד

מאת ר' יהודה בן שמואל החסיד

1 אַנְעִים זְמִירוֹת וְשִׁירִים אֶאֱרֹג
כִּי אֵלֶיךָ נַפְשִׁי תַעֲרֹג:

2 נַפְשִׁי חִמְּדָה בְּצֵל יָדֶךָ
לָדַעַת כָּל־רָז סוֹדֶךָ:

3 מִדֵּי דַבְּרִי בִּכְבוֹדֶךָ
הוֹמֶה לִבִּי אֶל דּוֹדֶיךָ:

4 עַל־כֵּן אֲדַבֵּר בְּךָ נִכְבָּדוֹת
וְשִׁמְךָ אֲכַבֵּד בְּשִׁירֵי יְדִידוֹת:

5 אֲסַפְּרָה כְבוֹדְךָ וְלֹא רְאִיתִיךָ
אֲדַמְּךָ אֲכַנְּךָ וְלֹא יְדַעְתִּיךָ:

6 בְּיַד נְבִיאֶיךָ בְּסוֹד עֲבָדֶיךָ
דִּמִּיתָ הֲדַר כְּבוֹד הוֹדֶךָ:

7 גְּדֻלָּתְךָ וּגְבוּרָתֶךָ
כִּנּוּ לְתֹקֶף פְּעֻלָּתֶךָ:

38

8 דִּמּוּ אוֹתָךְ וְלֹא כְּפִי יֶשְׁךָ
וַיְשַׁוּוּךָ לְפִי מַעֲשֶׂיךָ׃

9 הַמְשִׁילוּךָ בְּרֹב חֶזְיוֹנוֹת
הִנְּךָ אֶחָד בְּכָל־דִּמְיוֹנוֹת׃

10 וַיֶּחֱזוּ בְךָ זִקְנָה וּבַחֲרוּת
וּשְׂעַר רֹאשְׁךָ בְּשֵׂיבָה וְשַׁחֲרוּת׃

11 זִקְנָה בְּיוֹם דִּין וּבַחֲרוּת בְּיוֹם קְרָב
כְּאִישׁ מִלְחָמוֹת יָדָיו לוֹ רָב׃

12 חָבַשׁ כּוֹבַע יְשׁוּעָה בְּרֹאשׁוֹ
הוֹשִׁיעָה לּוֹ יְמִינוֹ וּזְרוֹעַ קָדְשׁוֹ׃

13 טַלְלֵי אוֹרוֹת רֹאשׁוֹ נִמְלָא
וּקְוֻצּוֹתָיו רְסִיסֵי לָיְלָה׃

14 יִתְפָּאֵר בִּי כִּי חָפֵץ בִּי
וְהוּא יִהְיֶה לִּי לַעֲטֶרֶת צְבִי׃

15 כֶּתֶם טָהוֹר פָּז דְּמוּת רֹאשׁוֹ
וְחַק עַל מֵצַח כְּבוֹד שֵׁם קָדְשׁוֹ׃

16 לְחֵן וּלְכָבוֹד צְבִי תִפְאָרָה
אֻמָּתוֹ לוֹ עִטְּרָה עֲטָרָה׃

17 מַחְלְפוֹת רֹאשׁוֹ כְּבִימֵי בְחֻרוֹת
קְוֻצּוֹתָיו תַּלְתַּלִּים שְׁחוֹרוֹת׃

18 נְוֵה הַצֶּדֶק בֵּית תִּפְאַרְתּוֹ
יַעֲלֶה נָּא עַל רֹאשׁ שִׂמְחָתוֹ׃

39

SPEAKING OF GOD

סְגֻלָּתוֹ תְּהִי בְיָדוֹ עֲטֶרֶת 19
וְצַנִּיף מְלוּכָה צְבִי תִּפְאֶרֶת:

עֲמוּסִים נְשָׂאָם עֲטֶרֶת עִנְּדָם 20
מֵאֲשֶׁר יָקְרוּ בְעֵינָיו כִּבְּדָם:

פְּאָרוֹ עָלַי וּפְאֵרִי עָלָיו 21
וְקָרוֹב אֵלַי בְּקָרְאִי אֵלָיו:

צַח וְאָדוֹם לִלְבוּשׁוֹ אָדֹם 22
פּוּרָה בְּדָרְכוֹ בְּבוֹאוֹ מֵאֱדוֹם:

קֶשֶׁר תְּפִלִּין הֶרְאָה לֶעָנָו 23
תְּמוּנַת יְיָ לְנֶגֶד עֵינָיו:

רוֹצֶה בְעַמּוֹ עֲנָוִים יְפָאֵר 24
יוֹשֵׁב תְּהִלּוֹת בָּם לְהִתְפָּאֵר:

רֹאשׁ דְּבָרְךָ אֱמֶת קוֹרֵא מֵרֹאשׁ דּוֹר וָדוֹר 25
עַם דּוֹרֶשְׁךָ דְּרוֹשׁ:

שִׁית הֲמוֹן שִׁירַי נָא עָלֶיךָ 26
וְרִנָּתִי תִּקְרַב אֵלֶיךָ:

תְּהִלָּתִי תְּהִי לְרֹאשְׁךָ עֲטֶרֶת 27
וּתְפִלָּתִי תִּכּוֹן קְטֹרֶת:

תִּיקַר שִׁירַת רָשׁ בְּעֵינֶיךָ 28
כַּשִּׁיר יוּשַׁר עַל קָרְבָּנֶיךָ:

בִּרְכָתִי תַעֲלֶה לְרֹאשׁ מַשְׁבִּיר 29
מְחוֹלֵל וּמוֹלִיד צַדִּיק כַּבִּיר:

40

30 וּבְבִרְכָתִי תְּנַעֲנַע לִי רֹאשׁ
וְאוֹתָהּ קַח־לְךָ כִּבְשָׂמִים רֹאשׁ:

31 יֶעֱרַב נָא שִׂיחִי עָלֶיךָ
כִּי נַפְשִׁי תַעֲרֹג אֵלֶיךָ:

2 HYMN OF THE GLORY
by Judah ben Samuel Heḥasid

1 I sing sweet hymns and weave together songs,
  Since but for You my panting soul still longs.

2 My soul desires to be under the shadow of Your hand
  That it may of all Your secrets the meaning understand.

3 When of Your glory I but speak
  My heart is stirred Your love to seek.

4 Thus while some weighty things of You I shall proclaim,
  It is with songs of love that I honor Your name.

5 Your glory I shall tell, though I have never seen You.
  I know not what You are, but image can describe You.

6 Through Your prophets and in Your servants' mystic speech
  You let us a mere likeness of Your glory reach.

7 Your greatness and Your power, too, they named
  But after Your works for which You are famed.

8 They visioned You not in Your absolute.
  Your deeds alone vouchsafed them Your similitude.

9 In different visions their analogies came.
  But, for all their similes, You remain the same.

10 They saw You ancient, and they saw You young.
   As both white hair and black upon Your head was hung.

11 Old age in judgment, youth on a fighting day
   When, as a warrior, His hands the battle sway.

41

12 Salvation's helmet on His head He wore;
His right hand and His holy arm the victory Him bore.

13 His head replete with saving dew of light,
His curls still wet with dewdrops of the night.

14 Glorified by me since He delights in me,
A crown of beauty He'll ever be for me.

15 The image of His head appears like fine pure gold;
Engraved upon His brow, His holy name is told.

16 For grace and glory, for splendor and renown
His chosen people made for Him a crown.

17 His head of plaited hair like that of youthful time;
His locks flow in black curls as they do in one's prime.

18 The place of justice, His Temple's glorious site,
O may He set it above His chief delight.

19 A diadem in His hand His treasured folk shall be,
Of beauty and of splendor a crown for royalty.

20 The people that were borne by Him, a crown for them He
bound.
He honored them, for in His sight so precious they were found.

21 His glory rests on me, my glory upon Him;
And He is near to me when I call out to Him.

22 He is bright and ruddy, all red appears His dress,
When He comes home from Edom, from treading the
winepress.

23 The knot of the *tephillin* to Moses He has shown.
The meek one had this vision as he stood there alone.

24 Delighting in His people, He glorifies the meek,
Enthroned above their praises, His glory there to seek.

25 Truth is Your word's beginning, thence every age's call;
The people for You questing, You, too, quest for them all!

26 My many songs, I pray, place on Yourself on high,
And let my cry of joy approach You very nigh.

27 My praise shall be for You a crown upon Your head,
And as the incense was of old, the prayer I have said.

28 As precious as in days of yore the song of priestly rite
So may my own poor song appear as precious in Your sight.

29 My blessing, may it now ascend to God who all sustains,
Creator, Father, Righteous One, Almighty He remains.

30 And, at my humble blessing, to me Your head incline,
And grant it Your acceptance as though to spices fine.

31 O let this prayerful musing be sweet to You as songs,
Since only for Your nearness my panting soul yet longs.

Commentary

The text of this poem may be found in *The Authorised Daily Prayer Book*, ed. Simeon Singer, 15th ed., London, 1935, pp. 78–80. Its listing in Davidson's *Thesaurus* is in vol. 1, p. 310, no. 6827. Its author is generally taken to be Rabbi Judah ben Samuel Heḥasid of Regensburg (*ca.* 1150–1217). See the sources quoted in S. Baer, ed., *Seder 'Abhodath Yisrael*, Berlin, 1937, p. 250; and cf. Abraham Berliner, *Der Einheitsgesang*, Berlin, 1910, p. 13. Elie Munk (*The World of Prayer*, vol. 2, New York, 1963, p. 60), among others, would attribute the poem to Judah's father, Samuel. He bases himself on stanza 28 where, in the word *rash*, he sees an abbreviation of Rabbi *Sh*emuel. But this seems somewhat far-fetched, since the poet would hardly refer to himself by his honorific title while omitting his patronymic.

Stanzas 5 through 27 form a complete alphabetical acrostic. The poem has meter and rhyme, the latter being achieved by having the two stichoi of each stanza end with the same syllable.

Issachar Jacobson (*Nethibh Binah*, vol. 2, Tel-Aviv, 1968, pp. 262ff.) has pointed out that, while stanzas 1 through 10

43

address God in the second person, stanzas 11 through 24 refer to
God in the third person, the rest of the poem, stanzas 25 through
31, reverting to the second person. Jacobson tries to explain this
grammatical peculiarity by saying, on the basis of the 'Glory
theology' of the German Pietists, that the stanzas in the second
person are addressed to God Himself, while the stanzas in the
third person speak about the 'Glory.' In this manner, according
to Jacobson, the poet wanted to reduce the force of the anthropomorphisms. There is something suggestive about this view,
since something seems obviously to be intended by the change
from the second person to the third person, and back again to the
second person. But it may be argued against Jacobson that, in the
first place, given the general orientation of the German Pietists,
the author of the poem would have felt no need to 'reduce' the
force of the anthropomorphisms. Moreover, stanzas 10, 27, and
30 are hardly any less anthropomorphic in content and expression
than stanzas 11 through 24.

1 *for You my panting soul still longs.* Based on Psalm 42:2, 'As the
hart pants after the water brooks, so pants my soul after You, O
God.'
10-13 If the Song of Songs be understood as describing the love
between God and Israel, and the Rabbis so understood it, then the
qualities and attributes of the young lover in the Song of Songs
must be regarded as the attributes of God. That would include
such descriptions as the 'head filled with dew . . . locks with the
drops of the night' (Song 5:2), and 'locks are curled, and black as
a raven' (Song 5:10). On the other hand, the author of the Book
of Daniel also purports to give an intimation of the Divine when
he describes the 'Ancient of Days' as having hair 'like pure wool,'
i.e., white (Daniel 7:9). The Rabbis, in such passages as *Mekhilta,
Bahodesh*, par. 5 (ed. Horovitz-Rabin, pp. 219-20) and b. Ḥagigah
14a, insist that the descriptions of 'youth' and 'old age' refer to
the same One God, and that this One God reveals Himself under
different aspects, depending upon the circumstances. God waging
Israel's battles conjures up the image of youth, whereas God
functioning as a teaching elder, as at Sinai, or as a judge in Daniel's

vision, is seen under the aspect of old age. The poet here affirms both aspects of the Deity, following in the tradition of the Rabbinic passages mentioned.

12 *Salvation's helmet.* Cf. Isaiah 59:17.

His right hand, etc. A direct quotation from Psalm 98:1.

13 *saving dew of light.* Based on Isaiah 26:19—a very difficult verse linguistically. This much, however, is certain: that the verse links 'dew,' 'light,' and an eschatological Resurrection.

15 *like fine pure gold.* Cf. Song of Songs 5:11—again, part of the description of the young lover.

Engraved upon His brow. Gerald Friedlander (*Pirké de Rabbi Eliezer,* London, 1916, p. 22, n. 12) finds the source of that somewhat obscure statement in *Pirqé deRabbi Eliezer,* chapter 4, where God is described as wearing a crown on His head, 'and the Ineffable Name is upon His forehead.'

16 *His chosen people made for Him a crown.* The 'crown' which the poet has in mind is the 'crown' wrought out of Israel's prayers. Cf. *Exodus Rabbah* 21:4. The particular terminology here used by the poet is based upon a rather involved piece of Rabbinic exegesis found in *Pesiqta deRabh Kahana, pisqa* 1 (ed. Buber, pp. 4a, b). Commenting on the words, 'the crown wherewith his mother has crowned him' (Song of Songs 3:11), Rabbi Isaac said that there was no indication in the Bible that Bathsheba had made a crown for Solomon. Consequently, the verse cannot refer to Solomon and his mother, which—if Solomon stands for God—leaves the implication that the crown was made for God. But by whom? Rabbi Eleazar, the son of Rabbi Yosé, attempts to solve this difficulty by quoting an explanation he had heard from his father. It is based upon the defective spelling of *le-ummi* ('my nation') in Isaiah 51:4. The word can, therefore, be read as *le-immi* ('to my mother')—'mother' and 'nation' thus becoming identified. If, then, it be granted that the 'Solomon' of Song of Songs is God, it would follow from Song of Songs 3:11 that Israel, God's nation, had made a crown for Him. And that is the terminology here employed by the poet.

17 Cf. the commentary on stanzas 10–13.

18 *The place of justice.* Cf. Jeremiah 31:23, where the 'habitation of righteousness' is in apposition to the 'mountain of holiness,' i.e., the Temple mount.

His Temple's glorious site. The current editions of the prayerbook read *tzebhi thiph-arto,* i.e., 'the beauty of His glory,' which, in this context, would in any case refer to the Temple. However, S. Baer (op. cit., p. 251) quotes an old printed edition which reads *beth tiph-arto,* i.e., 'the house of His glory,' which makes the reference to the Temple even more explicit. We have adopted that reading.

O may He set it. For the wording and the sentiment, see Psalm 137:6.

19 *A diadem in His hand.* Cf. Isaiah 62:3.

22 *He is bright and ruddy.* Cf. Song of Songs 5:10. The rest of this stanza uses the terminology of Isaiah 63:1–3, where God's vengeance against Edom, Israel's arch-enemy, is expressed in the imagery of God's treading the winepress of Edom.

23 *The knot of the* tephillin, *etc.* The Hebrew original does not mention Moses by name, but speaks of 'the meek one'. Cf. Numbers 12:3. The image itself is based on b. *Berakhoth* 7a. Commenting on Exodus 33:20–3 ('And He said: "You cannot see My face . . . And I will take away My hand, and you shall see My back . . ." '), R. Ḥama bar Bizana said in the name of R. Simeon Ḥasida: 'This teaches us that the Holy One, praised be He, showed Moses the knot of the phylacteries.' Since, on the same page of the Talmud, God is described as actually wearing phylacteries Himself, the reference to the 'knot of the *tephillin*' could almost be taken literally—once allowance for that kind of anthropomorphism is made. However, there was a tendency among the medieval commentators to soften the impact of that particular anthropomorphism by interpreting the 'knot of the *tephillin*' as the 'interrelatedness of all existing things and their dependence upon divine providence.' See Jacob Ibn Ḥabib's commentary on his *'Eyn Ya'aqobh,* ad loc.

25 *Truth is Your word's beginning.* A quotation from Psalm 119:160.

26 *place on Yourself.* Since the prayers and the praises constitute the 'crown' (see stanzas 16 and 27), the poet's Hebrew, *shith . . .*

'alekha, can be rendered only in this way—although practically all modern translators shy away from this literalism.

28 *the song of priestly rite*. Literally: 'the song which was sung at Your sacrifices.'

my own poor song. Literally: 'the song of the poor man.' Munk's suggestion that *rash*, the Hebrew word for 'poor man,' is an abbreviation for 'Rabbi Samuel' (Judah Heḥasid's father) has already been noted.

30 *to me Your head incline*. For the image of 'God inclining His head' as a sign of divine approval, see b. *Berakhoth* 7a.

31 *Since only for Your nearness, etc*. The identical Hebrew words from Psalm 42:2, though differently arranged, as in the second line of the first stanza. The poem thus ends as it begins with the mystical longing of the poet.

CHAPTER IV

'On Account of our Sins'

The traditional Jewish response to adversity has, on the whole, always taken the form of self-blame and self-accusation. Suffering, it was felt, must be the result of sin. The Book of Job did, of course, eloquently argue against such a notion; and, in the case of *individual* suffering, the lesson of the Book of Job may, on occasion, have been taken to heart. But when it came to the suffering of the Jewish people as a whole, to the destruction of Temple and state, to the intolerable conditions of exile, to the burnings of Jewish books and of Jewish lives, to pogroms and to persecutions, the standard reaction has always been: 'On account of our sins we were exiled from our land, and far removed from our soil.'[1] Every new persecution brought new fast days and new penitential prayers—new admissions of the conviction that God remained far from Israel on account of Israel's continuous sins.

That attitude is well reflected in poem no. 3, which may already have been included in the very first Jewish prayerbook, the ninth-century *Seder Rabh 'Amram Gaon*.[2] 'More guilty are we than all other peoples,' it begins; and it ends by saying: 'But we still have not turned from our error!' Leopold Zunz devoted his great work on the synagogal poetry of the middle ages[3] largely to the great number of penitential poems which were composed in medieval times. It is quite in accord with the type of devotional literature he catalogued in that volume that Zunz prefaced his technical discussion by a chapter devoted to 'The Sufferings.'[4]

48

The connection is clear. Without those sufferings, the vast literature of penitential poems would not have arisen. And the obverse of this, the medieval Jewish response to persecution and suffering, was penitence!

Only in the nineteenth century was that whole attitude called into question—and then primarily because nascent Reform Judaism, child of the emancipation, found no existential meaning in the concept of 'exile.' Diaspora existence, for Reform Judaism, was not punitive exile on account of Israel's sins, but rather the inevitable consequence of Israel's glorious mission to be a 'light unto the nations.' With the concept of 'exile' thus banished from its theology, Reform Judaism also had to revise those liturgical expressions which linked diaspora existence to Israel's sins.

The 1819 prayerbook of the Hamburg Temple still retained the traditional formulation, 'On account of our sins we were exiled from our land,' although it omitted the subsequent petition that Israel be restored to its land. A few other Reform liturgies followed the Hamburg model. By 1866, however, Joseph Aub had so revised the formula in his edition of the prayerbook that it now read: 'On account of their sins our fathers were exiled from their land, and far removed from their soil.' Both the concept of 'exile' as such, and of the connection between 'exile' and sin, had thus been retained. Yet the worshipper was no longer personally involved. The ancestors had sinned, and the ancestors were exiled.

Aub's Berlin congregants in 1866 were no longer living 'in exile.' The 1881 prayerbook of the Berlin New Synagogue went one step further. It still, in Aub's phraseology, admitted the fact that 'our fathers were exiled from their land, and far removed from their soil.' But it no longer connected that historical event with any sins which the ancestors might have committed. Instead, the prayer goes on to say: 'You have scattered us throughout the countries to sanctify Your Name in the world, from the rising of the sun unto the going down thereof.'

By 1905, the proposed prayerbook of Baden (which, however, was never officially adopted), while still speaking of the ancestors who were exiled from their land, substituted the phrase, 'on account of Your holy plan,' for the traditional 'on account of our sins' (or Aub's 'on account of their sins'), and proceeded to enlarge upon the theme of the Mission of Israel. That was probably the very last attempt to mention the *ancestral* exile, even in the very attenuated forms noted here, which was made in the liturgy of Reform Judaism. In the meantime, other Reform prayerbooks had omitted that paragraph altogether—a procedure which was also adopted by all subsequent prayer manuals of Liberal and Reform Judaism.[5]

While, in terms of the self-awareness of nineteenth-century Reform Jews, this rejection of the concept of 'exile' is perfectly understandable, it nevertheless raises a question with which the thinkers of Reform Judaism do not seem to have dealt. More than any other variety of modern Judaism, Reform Judaism claimed to stand in direct succession to the Hebrew Prophets. Yet the doctrine that 'we were exiled on account of our sins' is not a doctrine which was invented by Pharisaic or medieval Judaism. It is, in fact, a doctrine which is based on one of the more prominent teachings of the Hebrew Prophets. When disaster threatened, and when calamity came upon the Jewish people, the biblical Prophets did not so much blame the great powers of their time—Egypt, Assyria, and Babylon. They taxed their own Jewish contemporaries with having, through their sins, induced God to use those great powers as 'the rod of His anger.' Indeed, it might be argued that the religious views of the Prophets gained currency among the people only after the threatened destructions had come to pass. To that extent, therefore, the traditional Jewish posture of reacting to persecution with penitence may be said to constitute an authentic element of Prophetic religion; and it remains one of the innumerable ironies of religious history that those who, more than all other Jews, claimed to represent the religion of the Prophets in the nineteenth century found it necessary to remove that element of Prophetic teaching which had always been a striking component of Jewish worship.

There was very little common ground between Reform Judaism, in its so-called 'classical' period, and its contemporary, the rising Jewish nationalist movement which evolved into Zionism.

If the former no longer found any meaning in the concept of 'exile,' the latter was very much obsessed by it. But Zionism was obsessed by 'exile' only because it wanted, once and for all, to put an end to that deplorable condition. Although few in either movement may have been aware of it at the time, both Zionism and Reform Judaism engaged in a common Promethean assault upon the traditional sin–exile–redemption syndrome. Neither was willing any longer to maintain the traditional passive attitude of waiting for the Messiah. Both emphasized, albeit in different ways, man's role in bringing about his own salvation. And the theological presupposition that sin is the cause of 'exile' was explicitly or implicitly rejected by both.

As far as Zionism is concerned, the implicit was made explicit in the words of the poet laureate of the national rebirth, Ḥayyim Naḥman Bialik (1873–1934). Bialik visited Kishinev, as a member of the Odessa Jewish Historical Commission, after the pogroms of 1903. A year later, still under the impact of what he had seen and heard in Kishinev, he wrote 'In the City of Slaughter.' In that poem, Bialik describes in gory detail, which leaves nothing to the imagination, the course and the effects of the Kishinev pogroms. Towards the end, he turns his attention to the survivors. He finds them gathered in their synagogue, engaged in the rites of the fast day liturgy, and beating their breasts while reciting the traditional confession of sins. At that point, the poet has God Himself react in the following outburst:[6]

> And see them beating on their hearts, confessing
> > their iniquity
> By saying: 'We have sinned, betrayed!' Their heart
> > believes not what they say.
> A shattered vessel, can it sin? Can potsherds
> > have iniquity?
> Why, then, their praying unto Me?—Speak unto them,
> > and let them storm!
> Let them lift up their fist at Me, resent the insult
> > done to them,
> Insult of ages, first and last;
> And let them smash the sky and My own throne
> > with their raised fist.

No passive submission to the recurring catastrophes of Jewish fate, no litanies of confession, and no reiteration of the old refrain about being exiled on account of our sins, but a call to rebellion against the exile mentality, against God Himself. That was the burden of Bialik's 'In the City of Slaughter,' even as it has always been one of the distinctive undertones of the modern Jewish national revival.

But if the theology of 'on account of our sins' could no longer do justice to the pogroms at the beginning of this century, what are we to say about the Holocaust? Dealing with the doctrine of 'on account of our sins' in relation to the Holocaust, Emil L. Fackenheim writes:[7]

> Yet, suspend it we must. For however we twist and turn this doctrine in response to Auschwitz, it becomes a religious absurdity and even a sacrilege . . . Not a single one of the six million died because they had failed to keep the divine-Jewish covenant: they all died because their great-grandparents *had* kept it, if only to the minimum extent of raising Jewish children . . . Here is the rock on which the 'for our sins are we punished' suffers total shipwreck.

Similarly, Eliezer Berkovits comments:[8]

> Looking at the entire course of Jewish history, the idea that all this has befallen us because of our sins is an utterly unwarranted exaggeration . . . Nor do we for a single moment entertain the thought that what happened to European Jewry in our generation was divine punishment for sins committed by them. It was injustice absolute; injustice countenanced by God.

While Fackenheim and Berkovits challenge the applicability of certain traditional doctrines and theodicies to the Holocaust, they maintain their faith in Israel's God—in spite of the Holocaust. Richard L. Rubenstein, however, has come to the conclusion that 'Jewish history has written the final chapter in the terrible story of the God of history.'[9] Few modern Jewish theologians have joined Rubenstein in that radical conclusion; but, as one of the possible outcomes of the rejection of the 'on account of our sins' theology, it has its significance.

We see, then, that, during the nineteenth and twentieth

centuries, and for a variety of reasons, a doctrine which has held sway during the previous eighteen centuries was both challenged and, in some quarters, rejected. Perhaps this was not the least of the transformations which Judaism has undergone in the modern period. The fact, however, that we are able to associate the challenges so closely with the last two centuries only underlines the seemingly undisputed acceptance of that doctrine in earlier periods.

אשמנו מכל עם

מאת רב עמרם גאון (?)

1	אָשַׁמְנוּ מִכָּל־עָם
2	בֹּשְׁנוּ מִכָּל־דּוֹר
3	גָּלָה מִמֶּנּוּ מָשׂוֹשׂ
4	דָּוָה לִבֵּנוּ בַּחֲטָאֵינוּ
5	הֶחְבַּל אֱוִיֵּנוּ
6	וְנִפְרַע פְּאֵרֵנוּ
7	זְבוּל בֵּית מִקְדָּשֵׁנוּ
8	חָרַב בַּעֲוֹנֵינוּ
9	טִירָתֵנוּ הָיְתָה לְשַׁמָּה
10	יְפִי אַדְמָתֵנוּ לְזָרִים
11	כֹּחֵנוּ לְנָכְרִים
12	וַעֲדַיִן לֹא שַׁבְנוּ מִטָּעוּתֵנוּ:
13	לְעֵינֵינוּ עָשְׁקוּ עֲמָלֵנוּ
14	מִמְשָׁךְ וּמוֹרָט מִמֶּנּוּ
15	נָתְנוּ עֻלָּם עָלֵינוּ
16	סָבַלְנוּ עַל שִׁכְמֵנוּ
17	עֲבָדִים מָשְׁלוּ בָנוּ
18	פֶּרֶק אֵין מִיָּדָם

53

צָרוֹת רַבּוֹת סְבָבוּנוּ 19

קְרָאנוּךְ יְיָ אֱלֹהֵינוּ 20

רָחַקְתָּ מִמֶּנוּ בַּעֲוֹנֵינוּ 21

שַׁבְנוּ מֵאַחֲרֶיךָ 22

תָּעִינוּ וְאָבָדְנוּ 23

וַעֲדַיִן לֹא שַׁבְנוּ מִטָּעוּתֵנוּ : 24

3 'MORE GUILTY ARE WE'
by Rabh 'Amram Gaon (?)

1 More guilty are we than all other peoples,
2 More ashamed than all other generations.
3 Mirth has departed from us.
4 Our heart is faint because of our sins.
5 Our desires have been ruined,
6 Our glory dishevelled.
7 The habitation of our sanctuary
8 Has been devastated on account of our iniquities.
9 Our encampment has become a desolation.
10 The beauty of our soil belongs to strangers,
11 Our might to foreigners.
12   But we still have not turned from our error!
13 Before our eyes have we been robbed of the fruit of our labor,
14 Torn and stripped has it been from us.
15 They have placed their yoke upon us,
16 We are bearing it upon our shoulder.
17 Slaves rule over us;
18 There is none to deliver us from their hand.
19 Many troubles are encompassing us.
20 We have called upon You, O Lord, our God;
21 Yet You are far from us on account of our sins.
22 We have turned away from following You.
23 We went astray and we are lost.
24   But we still have not turned from our error!

Commentary

The text of this poem may be found in *Seder Haselihoth Keminhag Polin*, ed. E. D. Goldschmidt, Jerusalem, 5725, pp. 12–13. Its listing in Davidson's *Thesaurus* is in vol. 1, p. 367, no. 8115. Although there is no certainty about the prayer texts in the printed editions of *Seder Rabh 'Amram Gaon*, it is likely that this poem, a *selihah* (penitential prayer), was already a part of this ninth-century prayerbook. See *Seder Rabh 'Amram Gaon*, ed. E. D. Goldschmidt, Jerusalem, 1971, p. 153.

The structure, a simple alphabetical acrostic without rhyme, has a refrain in lines 12 and 24 which interrupts and supplements the alphabetical sequence in the middle and at the end.

The text is self-explanatory. It consists of biblical vocabulary and syntax. The biblical sources on which the various phrases in this poem are based are given by Goldschmidt in his edition of the *Seder Haselihoth*.

CHAPTER V

'Measure for Measure'

Was the doctrine of 'on account of our sins' really as generally accepted and undisputed in the pre-modern period as one might infer from the conclusion of our last chapter?

Discussing the effect of the destruction of Temple and state in the year 70 CE upon the early Rabbis, Richard L. Rubenstein argues that 'they were convinced that they and their contemporaries deserved the misfortunes which had befallen them.'[1] Rabbinic Judaism's all-powerful God would, of course, have been the most convenient object of blame for Jewish disaster, since He was ultimately responsible for what had happened. Nevertheless, from a psychological perspective, Rubenstein asserts that there would have been too much anxiety and tension in blaming God. Self-accusation may be bitter, but it is both safer and less anxiety-producing. The religious Jew of the Rabbinic period, then, had but two alternatives: 'He could blame himself for his misfortunes; or he could proclaim the death of the omnipotent Lord of history, reluctantly regarding the cosmos as hopelessly absurd and ultimately gratuitous, as did Elisha ben Abuya and as do such modern existentialists as Sartre and Camus.'[2]

Rubenstein himself, as we have already noted, opts for the second alternative, siding with Elisha ben Abuya, Sartre and Camus. But he describes Rabbinic Judaism as being totally committed to the first alternative. The people's suffering is to be understood as God's punitive retribution.

Bearing in mind the abundance of medieval penitential poems which enlarge upon the theme of 'on account of our sins' in response to specific instances of persecution, and remembering the rather recent origin of the outright challenges hurled against that doctrine, Rubenstein's view of the alternatives, and of Rabbinic Judaism's option, would seem to be conclusive.

But the matter is far more complicated than that. Not only do a number of medieval poems—some of which will be presented here—express a theology somewhat at variance with the theology expressed in the majority of the medieval penitential poems as well as with the theology imputed by Rubenstein to Rabbinic Judaism as a whole, but those exceptional poems are in many instances but poetic restatements of ideas first encountered within the Rabbinic literature itself.

It would seem, therefore, that Rubenstein has tended to over-simplify the situation by unnecessarily limiting the number of alternatives which, in fact, were available to the ancient Rabbis. We shall see presently what other alternatives there were, and how they have been utilized.

Poem no. 4, by Simeon bar Isaac bar Abun, a tenth-century poet living in the German city of Mainz,[3] reflects the poet's acceptance of the doctrine that national suffering is the result of the people's sins. Yet there is a marked difference between poem no. 3 and this poem by Simeon bar Isaac. The former is an un-mitigated rehearsal of the theme that the Jewish people deserve every single one of the misfortunes which have befallen them, because 'we still have not turned from our error.' But Simeon's poem, in spite of its lyrical use of a *leitmotif* taken from the Song of Songs, really contains a not so hidden accusation directed against God. *Some* suffering, the poet seems to be saying, un-doubtedly is deserved; but not *all* suffering. If we have committed such-and-such a sin, he says, then look, God, we have already been adequately punished by this-or-that suffering. The debt has been paid; the books have been balanced. Any further suffering is undeserved. Therefore, God, hasten to bring our sufferings to an end by rebuilding Jerusalem and fulfilling the messianic prophecies.

Simeon bar Isaac is thus a part of that time-honored Jewish

57

tradition which has found it possible to argue with God, and to hold Him to account by invoking that absolute justice by which God no less than man is bound. Abraham who, in Genesis 18: 23–32, argues against the indiscriminate destruction of the righteous together with the wicked may be seen as the prototype of the man who argues with God. 'Shall not the Judge of the whole world do justice?' (Genesis 18:25). That tradition is carried on by the Prophet Jeremiah. 'You have to be in the right, O Lord, if I argue with You!,' he said, 'Nevertheless I will bring certain cases to Your attention. Why does the way of guilty men prosper? Why are all they secure that deal treacherously?'[4]

The Book of Job is, of course, the outstanding example of man's argument with God; and, in more recent times, the eighteenth-century Rabbi Levi Isaac of Berditchev has become famous for pleading Israel's case against God.[5]

Rabbinic Judaism unhesitatingly maintained the view that God's retributive justice manifests itself in a 'measure for measure' ratio to man's actions—both for evil and for good.[6] 'With the measure with which a man measures, God measures to him.' If anything, God's mercy may, on occasion, make Him forgo the exacting of the full measure of punishment. But that God should punish beyond the deserved 'measure,' that would have been inconceivable to the Rabbis. It would have called into question God's justice.

Yet that is precisely how Simeon bar Isaac sees the present, though not the past, sufferings of Israel! What Israel is now suffering goes beyond any just application of the 'measure for measure' principle. Thus God is, as it were, obligated to bring about Israel's speedy redemption.

ברח דודי

מאת ר׳ שמעון בר יצחק בן אבון

1 בְּרַח דּוֹדִי אֶל שַׁאֲנַן נָוֶה.
2 וְאִם הִלְאָינוּ דֶּרֶךְ הַעֲוֶה.
3 הִנֵּה לָקִינוּ בְּכָל־מַדְוֶה.

וְאַתָּה יְיָ מָעוֹז וּמִקְוֶה. 4

עָלֶיךָ כָּל־הַיּוֹם נְקַוֶּה. 5

לְגָאֳלֵנוּ וּלְשִׂיתֵנוּ כְּגַן רָוֶה: 6

בָּרַח דּוֹדִי אֶל מְקוֹם מִקְדָּשֵׁנוּ. 7

וְאִם עֲוֹנוֹת עָבְרוּ רֹאשֵׁנוּ. 8

הִנֵּה בָאָה בַבַּרְזֶל נַפְשֵׁנוּ. 9

וְאַתָּה יְיָ גֹּאֲלֵנוּ קְדוֹשֵׁנוּ. 10

עָלֶיךָ נִשְׁפַּךְ שִׂיחַ רַחֲשֵׁנוּ. 11

לְגָאֳלֵנוּ מִמְּעוֹן קָדְשְׁךָ לְהַחְפִּישֵׁנוּ: 12

בָּרַח דּוֹדִי אֶל עִיר צִדְקֵנוּ. 13

וְאִם לֹא שָׁמַעְנוּ לְקוֹל מַצְדִּיקֵינוּ. 14

הִנֵּה אֲכָלוּנוּ בְּכָל־פֶּה מַדִּיקֵינוּ. 15

וְאַתָּה יְיָ שֹׁפְטֵנוּ מְחֹקְקֵנוּ. 16

עָלֶיךָ נַשְׁלִיךְ יַהַב חֶלְקֵנוּ. 17

לְגָאֳלֵנוּ בְּהַשְׁקֵט וּבְבִטְחָה לְהַחֲזִיקֵנוּ: 18

בָּרַח דּוֹדִי אֶל וַעַד הַזְּבוּל. 19

וְאִם עָלֶךָ שָׁבַרְנוּ בְּלִי סָבוּל. 20

הִנֵּה לָקִינוּ בְּכָל־מִינֵי חִבּוּל. 21

וְאַתָּה יְיָ מְשַׂמֵּחַ אָבוּל. 22

עָלֶיךָ נַסְבִּיר לְהַתִּיר כָּבוּל. 23

לְגָאֳלֵנוּ לְהִתְגַּדֵּל מֵעַל לִגְבוּל: 24

בָּרַח דּוֹדִי אֶל נְשָׂא מִגְּבָעוֹת. 25

וְאִם זַדְנוּ בִּפְרֹעַ פְּרָעוֹת. 26

הִנֵּה הִשִּׂיגֻנוּ צָרוֹת רַבּוֹת וְרָעוֹת. 27

וְאַתָּה יְיָ אֵל לְמוֹשָׁעוֹת. 28

עָלֶיךָ נִשְׁפַּךְ שִׂיחַ שַׁוְעוֹת. 29

לְגָאֳלֵנוּ וּלְעַטְּרֵנוּ כּוֹבַע יְשׁוּעוֹת: 30

4 'HASTEN, MY BELOVED'
by Simeon b. Isaac b. Abun

1 Hasten, my Beloved, to the tranquil site.
2 If we have wearied You by making our way perverse,
3 Then see, we have been smitten by every painful hurt.
4 But You, O Lord, are our refuge and our hope.
5 In You we hope the whole day long
6 That You will redeem us and make us like a watered garden.

7 Hasten, my Beloved, to our sanctuary's place.
8 If sins have risen far above our head,
9 Then see, our life by iron chains beset.
10 But You, O Lord, are our Holy One and Redeemer.
11 To You we pour forth our whispered plea
12 That You will redeem us from Your holy habitation,
     and set us free.

13 Hasten, my Beloved, to our Righteous City.
14 If we have not hearkened to the voices bidding us do right,
15 Then see, those who would crush us have consumed us
     with an open mouth.
16 But You, O Lord, are our Judge and Legislator.
17 Upon You we cast the burden of our fate
18 That You will redeem us and, with calm and trust,
     will make us strong.

19 Hasten, my Beloved, to our meeting's habitation.
20 If we have broken Your yoke, unborne,
21 Then see, we have been smitten with every kind of wound.
22 But You, O Lord, can make the mourner glad.
23 In You we hope that You will release the bound,
24 That You will redeem us and be exalted beyond
     Israel's border.

25 Hasten, my Beloved, to the mountain exalted above the hills.
26 If we have wilfully sinned by breaking all restraints,
27 Then see, many and grievous troubles have overtaken us.

28 But You, O Lord, are the God of salvation.
29 To You we pour forth our prayerful cries
30 That You will redeem us and crown us with the helmet
        of salvation.

Commentary

The text of this poem may be found in Arthur Davis and Herbert M. Adler, eds, *Service of the Synagogue*, Passover volume, 13th ed., London, 1949, p. 218. Its listing in Davidson's *Thesaurus* is in vol. 2, p. 76, no. 1692. It is a *ge-ullah* (a poem inserted into the benediction after the *Shema'*) for the morning service of the Sabbath during Passover week.

With some exceptions—notably the opening line of each of the five stanzas—there are four words to each line. Each stanza has its own rhyme. The first letters of the fourth word in the first line of each stanza, taken together, spell the name of the poet: Simeon. About Simeon b. Isaac b. Abun, who lived in Mainz in the tenth century, see Leopold Zunz, *Literaturgeschichte der synagogalen Poesie*, Berlin, 1865, pp. 111–15, 235–8; A. M. Habermann, in his edition of *Liturgical Poems of R. Shim'on bar Yiṣḥaq* (Hebrew), Berlin, 1938, pp. 7–18; and idem, in *Encyclopaedia Judaica*, vol. 14, col. 1551.

The opening words of each stanza, 'Hasten, my Beloved,' are a quotation from Song of Songs 8:14. The Song of Songs is the Scroll (*megillah*) traditionally read on the Festival of Passover. In the Rabbinic interpretation of this biblical book, the Song of Songs speaks about the love between God and Israel. Hence 'my Beloved' in this poem refers to God.

The fourth and fifth words of the first line of each stanza make up a synonym for Jerusalem and/or the Temple, based on verses from the Book of Isaiah.

1 *the tranquil site.* Or 'peaceful habitation,' as in Isaiah 33:20.
6 *like a watered garden.* Cf. Isaiah 58:11, 'and you shall be like a watered garden.'

7 *our sanctuary's place.* Cf. Isaiah 60:13, 'to beautify the place of My sanctuary.'

13 *our Righteous City.* Cf. Isaiah 1:16, 'Afterwards you shall be called The city of righteousness.'

19 *our meeting's habitation.* Cf. Isaiah 63:15, 'Look down from Your holy and glorious habitation.'

24 *be exalted beyond Israel's border.* The Hebrew original, for reasons of rhyme, does not contain the word 'Israel.' But it is clear that the poet wants us to think of Malachi 1:5, 'And you shall say: "The Lord is great beyond the border of Israel." '

25 *the mountain exalted above the hills.* Cf. Isaiah 2:2, 'the mountain of the Lord's house . . . shall be exalted above the hills.' Actually, the poet omits the word 'mountain'. He merely refers to 'exalted above the hills.'

26 *by breaking all restraints.* The Hebrew text has *biphro'a pera'oth,* words taken from Judges 5:2. The meaning of the biblical text is disputed. The *Targum* renders: 'When the house of Israel had rebelled against the Torah.' Rashi takes the words to mean: 'When breaches had been made in Israel.' Modern exegetes offer their own solution to the problem. Our translation assumes the poet's acceptance of the traditional interpretations.

CHAPTER VI

Tamar's Pledge

If Simeon bar Isaac based his claim on the Rabbinic 'measure for measure' principle, the Spanish-Jewish poet, Judah Halevi (before 1075–1141), proceeds from an even more daring assumption. According to him, God appears to be in Israel's debt!

Poem no. 5 is, on the face of it, a prayer of praise and thanksgiving for the deliverance at the Sea of Reeds. But the memory of the past redemption feeds the hope for the redemption yet to come. We may note in passing that, in the Ashkenazi rite, poems no. 4 and no. 5, respectively by Simeon bar Isaac and Judah Halevi, occupy the identical place in the liturgy. Both of them are inserted into the benediction commemorating the Exodus from Egypt, which follows the *Shema'* of the morning service—Simeon's on the Sabbath during Passover week, and Judah Halevi's on the seventh day of Passover, the day which recalls Israel's passing through the Sea of Reeds.[1]

Adopting the metaphor introduced by such Prophets as Hosea[2] and Jeremiah,[3] and taken for granted in the Rabbinic interpretation of the Song of Songs, Judah Halevi sees the relationship between God and Israel as that of a marriage—with the Exodus-Sinai sequence marking the betrothal. But the marriage has come to grief, and the poet prays that God may 'marry her as once before, not to divorce her as of yore.'

That much, by way of commonly accepted exegesis, Judah Halevi could take for granted. Yet, when the poet wants God to

63

redeem Israel, not because of His great mercy, but because Israel is *entitled* to that redemption, then Halevi goes beyond the conventional attitude. The latter may be summarized in an old prayer which, at first, was intended for the Day of Atonement, but which, later, was placed at the beginning of the daily liturgy. 'Master of all the worlds! Not because of our righteousness do we lay our supplications before You, but because of Your abundant mercies. For what are we? What is our life? What is our piety? What is our righteousness?'[4] Contrary to the mood expressed in that prayer, Judah Halevi asks for redemption as a reward for Israel's faithfulness in keeping the commandments. He singles out two of them for special mention: circumcision and the ritual fringes on the four corners of the garment, which are particularly associated with the Passover theme—for reasons which will become apparent in our commentary on this poem.

But Judah Halevi goes even further than that. By way of referring to circumcision, 'God's seal in the flesh,' and the ritual fringes, Halevi uses words and phrases which, in a totally different context, occur in Genesis, chapter 38.

In that Genesis story, we are told that, after her first two husbands—both of them sons of Judah—had died, Judah urged his daughter-in-law, Tamar, to wait in her father's house until Judah's third son, Shela, would be old enough to marry her. Tamar complied with the request; but Judah did not see to it that the promised marriage took place.

Hearing of Judah's intended journey to Timnah, Tamar disguised herself as a harlot, met Judah on his way to Timnah, and agreed to let Judah spend the night with her. However, Judah found himself unable to pay there and then for the favors he had received. He promised to send his acquaintance of the night a kid of the goats from the flock as her reward. But, when Tamar demanded a pledge to make sure that the debt would be paid, Judah left with her his seal, his cord, and his staff.

However, when Judah sent the kid of the goats from the flock, his messenger was informed by the local inhabitants that there was no harlot at that place. In order to avoid scandal, Judah decided not to pursue the matter any further.

About three months later, Judah was told that his daughter-in-law was pregnant, and he inferred from this that she must have been unfaithful. Tamar was summoned by Judah, and condemned to be burnt.

At that point, Tamar produced Judah's seal, cord, and staff, telling her father-in-law: 'The father of my child is the man to whom these things belong. Discern now, whose are these, the signet, and the cords, and the staff.' Judah, recalling his broken promise, confessed: 'She is more righteous than I.'

By having Israel confront God with the 'signet' and the 'cords', Halevi has cast Israel in the role of Tamar. He does not go as far as explicitly casting God in the role of Judah; but no reader familiar with both Halevi's Hebrew original and the story of Genesis, chapter 38, can possibly miss the point—nor, by implication, God's unspoken confession that wronged Israel has the better of the argument.

יום ליבשה

מאת ר' יהודה הלוי

1 יוֹם לְיַבָּשָׁה נֶהֶפְכוּ מְצוּלִים.
2 שִׁירָה חֲדָשָׁה שִׁבְּחוּ גְאוּלִים:

3 הִטְבַּעְתָּ בְתַרְמִית.
4 רַגְלֵי בַת עֲנָמִית.
5 וּפַעֲמֵי שָׁלַמִּית.
6 יָפוּ בַּנְּעָלִים:

7 וְכָל־רוֹאֵי יְשׁוּרוּן.
8 בְּבֵית הוֹדִי יְשׁוֹרְרוּן.
9 אֵין כָּאֵל יְשָׁרוּן.
10 וְאוֹיְבֵינוּ פְּלִילִים:

11 דְּגָלַי כֵּן תָּרִים.
12 עַל הַנִּשְׁאָרִים.
13 וּתְלַקֵּט נִפְזָרִים.
14 כִּמְלַקֵּט שִׁבֳּלִים:

15 הַבָּאִים עִמְּךָ.
16 בִּבְרִית חוֹתָמְךָ.
17 וּמִבֶּטֶן לְשִׁמְךָ.
18 הֵמָּה נְמוֹלִים:

19 הַרְאֵה אוֹתוֹתָם.
20 לְכָל־רוֹאֵי אוֹתָם.
21 וְעַל כַּנְפֵי כְסוּתָם.
22 יַעֲשׂוּ גְדִילִים:

23 לְמִי זֹאת נִרְשֶׁמֶת.
24 הַכֶּר־נָא דְּבַר אֱמֶת.
25 לְמִי הַחֹתֶמֶת.
26 וּלְמִי הַפְּתִילִים:

27 וְשׁוּב שֵׁנִית לְקַדְּשָׁהּ.
28 וְאַל תּוֹסִיף לְגָרְשָׁהּ.
29 וְהַעֲלֵה אוֹר שִׁמְשָׁהּ.
30 וְנָסוּ הַצְּלָלִים:

31 יְדִידִים רוֹמֲמוּךָ.
32 בְּשִׁירָה קִדְּמוּךָ.
33 מִי כָמוֹךָ.
34 יְיָ בָּאֵלִים:

35 יוֹם לַיַּבָּשָׁה נֶהֶפְכוּ מְצוּלִים.
36 שִׁירָה חֲדָשָׁה שִׁבְּחוּ גְאוּלִים:

66

5 'THE DAY THE DEEP SEA TURNED'
by Judah Halevi

1 The day the deep sea turned to sod
2 A new song freed ones sang to God.

3 Because of her deceit,
4 You drowned Anamith's feet,
5 The while the steps of Shulammite
6 Were, in her sandals, a delight.

7 And all who Jeshurun divine
8 Shall sing amidst my glorious shrine:
9 'Jeshurun's God, beyond compare!'
10 Even our foes are judges fair.

11 My banners You will raise again
12 Over the people that remain.
13 You'll gather those dispersed in scorn
14 Like one who gathers sheaves of corn.

15 Your cov'nant's sign they proudly bear,
16 As with You the old pact they share;
17 And, from their mother's womb still fresh,
18 Your signet's cut into their flesh.

19 Their tokens You may show to all
20 Whose eyes upon Your people fall.
21 To their garb's corners, four to match,
22 They faithfully the cords attach.

23 Inscribed is this at whose behest?
24 Discern now; have the truth confessed:
25 Who may the signet's owner be?
26 And who can claim the cords from me?

27 Then marry her as once before,
28 Not to divorce her as of yore.
29 And let arise her sun's bright light,
30 Putting her shadows to the flight.

31 Those You befriend before You came
32 With exaltations of Your Name:
33 'Who, to whom men would might accord,
34 Can be compared to You, O Lord?'

35 The day the deep sea turned to sod
36 A new song freed ones sang to God.

Commentary

The text of this poem may be found in Arthur Davis and Herbert M. Adler, eds, *Service of the Synagogue*, Passover volume, 13th ed., London, 1949, pp. 228ff. Its listing in Davidson's *Thesaurus* is in vol. 2, p. 342, no. 1814. It is a *ge-ullah* (poem inserted into the benediction after the *Shema*') for the morning service of the seventh day of Passover, the day on which the Crossing through the Sea of Reeds is commemorated.

The poem has both rhyme and meter. The first letters of each stanza spell the poet's name: Judah Halevi. This Spanish-Jewish poet and philosopher was born before 1075 and died in 1141. See the various articles about him in the *Encyclopaedia Judaica*, vol. 10, cols 355–66.

4–5 *Anamith's feet*. According to the Table of Nations in Genesis 10:13, Mizraim, the eponymous ancestor of Egypt, 'begot Ludim and Anamim, and Lehabim, etc.' From 'Anamim,' the poet formed the feminine name of 'Anamith' as a kind of female incarnation of Egypt—to contrast with the female symbol of Israel the Shulammite, who in Song of Songs 7:1–2 is described as dancing, and to whom it is said there: 'How beautiful are your steps in sandals!' The Song of Songs is the Scroll (*megillah*) assigned for Passover reading.

7 *And all who Jeshurun divine*. Jeshurun is a poetic name for Israel, as in Deuteronomy 32:15, 35:5, etc.

9 *'Jeshurun's God, beyond compare!'* Literally: 'There is none like the God of Jeshurun,' or 'O Jeshurun, there is none like God.' A direct quotation from Deuteronomy 33:26.

10 *Even our foes are judges fair.* Literally: 'Even our enemies themselves being judges.' A direct quotation from Deuteronomy 32:12.

15-18 *Your cov'nant's sign.* There is a close association between Passover and circumcision. Cf. Exodus 12:43 ff. 'The Lord said to Moses and Aaron: This is the law of the passover offering: No stranger shall eat of it . . . If a stranger who dwells with you would offer the passover to the Lord, all his males must be circumcised; then he shall be admitted to offer it; he shall then be as a citizen of the country. But no uncircumcised person may eat of it.' According to Joshua, chapter 5, upon entry into the Promised Land, Joshua circumcised all those whose circumcision had to be postponed on account of the desert wanderings. After the whole people had been circumcised, the Passover was celebrated. This chapter of the Book of Joshua is the *haphtarah* (Prophetic Lesson) of the first day of Passover. In our translation, lines 15 and 16 have been transposed.

21-2 *They faithfully the cords attach.* Here, the poet chooses the terminology of Deuteronomy 22:12. The commandment of the ritual fringes (*tzitzith*) is likewise associated with Passover, since, in the major passage where it is ordained, Numbers 15:37 ff., the commandment is immediately followed by the statement: 'I am the Lord your God who brought you out of the land of Egypt.' Because of this juxtaposition, the whole passage, a component of the daily *Shema'*, was called 'The Exodus from Egypt.' Cf. *Mishnah Berakhoth* 1:5.

24-6 *Discern now; etc.* Literally: 'Discern now the matter of truth, whose is the signet, and whose are the cords'—almost a *verbatim* quotation from Genesis 38:25. There, the words are spoken by Tamar to Judah. That God would admit, as Judah did in that story (Genesis 38:26), 'She is more righteous than I am,' is implied, though not expressed, by the poet who, in the next stanza, presents God with a demand which is predicated upon God's acknowledgment that the signet and the cords are His.

29-30 *And let arise her sun's bright light, etc.* Literally: 'And cause the light of her sun to rise; and the shadows shall flee away.' The latter phrase is from Song of Songs 2:17 and 4:6.

33-4 '*Who, to whom men would might accord, etc.*' Literally: 'Who is like You, O Lord, among the gods?' or 'Who is like You, O Lord, among the mighty?' (Exodus 15:11). Our translation is, in part, suggested by the translation of that verse in the Liberal prayerbook, *Service of the Heart*, London, 1967, p. 34: 'Who is like You, O Lord, among the gods men worship?'

CHAPTER VII

The Silent God

Judah Halevi called God to account by means of clever literary allusions. The twelfth-century author of poem no. 6, Isaac bar Shalom, though far less artistic than Judah Halevi, is far more outspoken. In response to the persecutions of the year 1147, and to the fate of one Jewish community in particular, he not only cries out to God, in the words of Psalm 83:2, 'Do not keep silence!' He does not shrink from hurling at the silent God the accusation that there is none like Him among the dumb. Perhaps it was this daring exclamation which failed to win a place for this poem in most of the current printed editions of the Ashkenazi prayerbook.

Still, the accusation, which, to some sensitive ears, might seem to border on the blasphemous, is not original with Isaac bar Shalom. It does, in fact, go back to the Talmud itself. For, *pace* Richard L. Rubenstein, the ancient Rabbis, confronted by the tragedy which had befallen their people, were not at all unanimous either in apportioning all blame to their people or in shielding God from all reproach. A few illustrations may help to clarify this.

The first of the Eighteen Benedictions[1] invokes God as 'great, mighty, and awe-inspiring,' a phrase which goes back to Deuteronomy 10:17, and, therefore, as far as the Rabbis were concerned, reflects the attributes which Moses himself ascribed to the Deity. Now, the Rabbis noted that, in Jeremiah 32:17f., the attributes of 'great' and 'mighty' were mentioned, while the attribute of 'awe-inspiring' was omitted. On the other hand, Daniel 9:4 describes God as 'great' and 'awe-inspiring,' but fails to list 'mighty' as one of God's attributes.

This led the Rabbis to question the justification of Jeremiah's and Daniel's evident tampering with the list of attributes transmitted on the authority of Moses. They found the justification in the following manner:[2]

> Jeremiah came and said: 'Aliens are destroying His Temple. Where then, are His awe-inspiring deeds?' Therefore he omitted (in Jeremiah 32:17f.) the attribute of 'awe-inspiring.'
> Daniel came and said: 'Aliens are enslaving His sons. Where are his mighty deeds?' Therefore he omitted (in Daniel 9:4) the attribute of 'mighty.'

Yet, on the basis of Nehemiah 9:32, where God is called 'great, mighty, and awe-inspiring,' the Rabbis also concluded that the Men of the Great Assembly had restored the two attributes dropped by Jeremiah and Daniel. Indeed, according to Rabbi Joshua ben Levi, that Assembly was called 'great' precisely on account of that restoration. Moreover, the Men of the Great Assembly did so because they re-interpreted the meaning of those attributes, not because they denied the historical circumstances which had caused the omissions by Jeremiah and Daniel. God was now called 'mighty' because He succeeded in suppressing His wrath which would have interfered with the enemies' designs upon the Temple. He was now called 'awe-inspiring' because, without the awe He inspires among the nations of the world, the Jewish minority would have had no chance of survival.[3]

This, however, still leaves us with the question of how, in the first place, Jeremiah and Daniel could have abolished something which had been established by Moses. Rabbi Eleazar answers this question by saying: 'Since they knew that the Holy One, praised be He, insists on truth, they would not say untrue things about Him.'[4] Thus, according to Rabbi Eleazar, in spite of the later re-interpretation of the divine attributes by the Men of the Great Assembly, Jeremiah and Daniel, heeding the divine mandate of speaking the truth, were justified by the historical events of their time in not calling God mighty and awe-inspiring. They could not have truthfully done so—at least not if one bears in mind what the words 'mighty' and 'awe-inspiring' are commonly taken to signify.

If one considers that the Rabbis quoted in the above passage lived after the destruction of the *second* Temple, and that they were not primarily historians dealing with the events which had taken place about half a millennium before their time, one would have to conclude that those Rabbis more nearly reflect the attitudes encountered in the second and third centuries of the common era. And those attitudes, called forth by the destruction of the second Temple and the second Jewish commonwealth, included the denial of God's might and of His awe-inspiring character!

More akin to the purported re-interpretation of the divine attributes by the Men of the Great Assembly is a statement attributed to Abba Ḥanan, which the Talmud records in the course of its description of Titus' destruction of the second Temple. Commenting on Psalm 89:9, 'Who is a mighty one like unto You, O Lord?,' Abba Ḥanan said: 'Who is like You, mighty in self-restraint? You heard the blasphemy and the insults of that wicked man, but You kept silent!'[5]

It is in this connection that the Talmud also quotes a teaching of the School of Rabbi Ishmael which, by means of the addition of a single Hebrew consonant (changing the word *elim* to *illemim*), makes 'Who is like You, O Lord, among the gods?' (Exodus 15:11) read like 'Who is like You, O Lord, among the dumb?'[6]

It may remain an open question whether the School of Rabbi Ishmael understood that 'dumbness' in the sense which Abba Ḥanan gave to Psalm 89:9, or whether an even more daring theological thought was offered here.[7] But there can be no doubt that, when Isaac bar Shalom borrowed that teaching of the School of Rabbi Ishmael and coupled it with the refrain, 'Do not keep silence!,' he meant to express his impatience with the silent God who seemed to be utterly impervious to the desperate straits of His people.

אֵין כָּמוֹךָ בָּאִלְּמִים

מאת ר׳ יצחק בר שלום

אֵין כָּמוֹךָ בָּאִלְּמִים. 1
דּוֹמֵם וְשׁוֹתֵק לְמַעֲנִימִים. 2
צָרֵינוּ רַבִּים קָמִים. 3
בְּהִוָּסְדָם יַחַד לְגַדְּפֵנוּ. 4
אַיֵּה מַלְכְּכֶם חֵרְפוּנוּ. 5
לֹא שְׁכַחֲנוּ וְלֹא שִׁקַּרְנוּ. 6
אַל דֳּמִי לָךְ: 7

גְּרוּשִׁים מִן גֵּו גֵּאוּ. 8
וְעַמְּךָ בְּפֶרֶךְ דֻּכְּאוּ. 9
מְשַׂנְאֶיךָ רֹאשׁ נָשָׂאוּ. 10
דּוֹרְשֵׁי אוֹבוֹת וֶאֱלִילִים. 11
יֹאמְרוּ אוֹיְבֵינוּ פְּלִילִים. 12
מָה הַיְּהוּדִים הָאֻמְלָלִים. 13
אַל דֳּמִי לָךְ: 14

הָבוּ לָכֶם עֵצָה. 15
פֶּן תִּהְיוּ לְשִׁמְצָה. 16
הֵן לָרִיב וּמַצָּה. 17
וְאִם תִּהְיוּ כָמוֹנוּ. 18
לָנוּ תִּקְרְבוּ וְתִפְנוּ. 19
לְעַם אֶחָד וְהָיִינוּ. 20
אַל דֳּמִי לָךְ: 21

זָעֲקוּ לֹוקִים וַיַּעֲנוּ. 22
לֹא נָשׁוּב וְלֹא נַעַבְדֶנּוּ. 23
שֶׁקֶץ תְּשַׁקְּצֵנוּ וְתַעֵב תְּתַעֲבֶנּוּ. 24
חַי וְקַיָּם גָּאֲלֵנוּ. 25

74

26 אוֹתוֹ נַעֲבוֹד וּנְחַטְבֵנוּ.
27 בְּעֵת צָרָה יְשׁוּעָתֵנוּ.
28 אַל דֳּמִי לָךְ:
29 טְבוֹחַ יְלָדִים הֵכִינוּ.
30 בִּרְכַּת הַזֶּבַח כִּוֵּנוּ.
31 שְׁמַע יִשְׂרָאֵל יְיָ אֱלֹהֵינוּ
32 יְיָ אֶחָד וּנְיַחֲדֶנּוּ.
33 וְעַל קִדּוּשׁ שְׁמוֹ הֲרַגְנוּ.
34 לִנְפּוֹל בַּחֶרֶב נָשֵׁינוּ וְטַפֵּנוּ.
35 אַל דֳּמִי לָךְ:

36 כֹּהֲנִים לְזֶבַח עוֹלָתָם.
37 עָקְדוּ יְלָדִים וְאִמּוֹתָם.
38 וְשָׂרְפוּ בָאֵשׁ אֶת־עוֹרוֹתָם.
39 לִזְרוֹק דְּמֵי אֲחָיוֹת וְאַחִים.
40 וּלְקַטֵּר אִמּוּרֵי נִיחוֹחִים.
41 אֶת־הָרֹאשׁ וְאֶת־הַנְּתָחִים.
42 אַל דֳּמִי לָךְ:

43 מַעֲרָכָה גְדוּשָׁה שְׂזוּפָה.
44 כְּכִירָה לֹא קְטוּמָה וּגְרוּפָה.
45 וְכָל־בֵּית יִשְׂרָאֵל יִבְכּוּ אֶת־הַשְּׂרֵפָה.
46 נוֹפְלִים לְרִשְׁפֵּי שַׁלְהֶבֶת יָהּ.
47 נוֹעָדִים לִמְחִיצַת בְּנֵי עֲלִיָּה.
48 חֲנַנְיָה מִישָׁאֵל וַעֲזַרְיָה.
49 אַל דֳּמִי לָךְ:

50 סְחִי שָׂמוּ תּוֹרַת מֹשֶׁה.
51 וְתַלְמוּד רָבִינָא וְרַב אַשֵׁי.
52 הַעַל אֵלֶּה תִתְאַפַּק וְתֶחֱשֶׁה.
53 עַמּוּדִים וּגְוִילִים לַאֲבָחוֹת.

54 וְאֹתִיּוֹת קְדוֹשׁוֹת פּוֹרְחוֹת.
55 מִכְתַּב אֱלֹהִים חָרוּת עַל הַלֻּחוֹת.
56 אַל דֳּמִי לָךְ:

57 פָּסַע אוֹיֵב בְּוֶיךְ.
58 וְאָבַד טוֹבִי וְשָׁם לְאַיִן.
59 וַיַּהֲרוֹג כֹּל מַחֲמַדֵּי עַיִן.
60 צִיּוֹן לִפְרָט וַאֲרֶשֶׁת.
61 צָרָה אֶל אֲחוֹתָהּ נִגֶּשֶׁת.
62 הֵכִינוּ לִפְעָמַי רֶשֶׁת.
63 אַל דֳּמִי לָךְ:

64 קֵץ קָדוֹשׁ נַחְשׁוֹן.
65 נָגַע צָר בְּאִישׁוֹן.
66 בְּעֶשְׂרִים לַחֹדֶשׁ הָרִאשׁוֹן.
67 רֻטְּשׁוּ דּוֹרְשֵׁי חֲמוּרוֹת.
68 וְקַלּוֹת וְשָׁווֹת גְּזֵרוֹת.
69 הַחֻקִּים וְהַמִּשְׁפָּטִים וְהַתּוֹרוֹת.
70 אַל דֳּמִי לָךְ:

71 שַׁדַּי קַנָּא לְתוֹרָתֶךָ.
72 לְבַשׁ נִקְמָתְךָ וְקִנְאָתֶךָ.
73 וְעוֹרְרָה אֶת־גְּבוּרָתֶךָ.
74 גָּעַרְתָּ חַיַּת נוֹבֵר.
75 בְּכִלְיוֹן שׁוֹד וָשֶׁבֶר.
76 אוֹתוֹ וְאֶת־עַמּוֹ בַּדֶּבֶר.
77 אַל דֳּמִי לָךְ:

78 יְמִינְךָ רַהַב מַחַצְבֶת.
79 הָרֵץ גֻּלְגֹּלֶת בְּמַקֶּבֶת.
80 זֹאת עֲדִינָה הַיּוֹשָׁבֶת.

צַח וְאָדוֹם מִשֵּׂעִיר. 81

נְסוּכָה בְּכִלָּיוֹן תַּסְעִיר. 82

כְּאִישׁ מִלְחָמוֹת קִנְאָה תָעִיר. 83

אַל דֳּמִי לָךְ : 84

קַנֵּה שֵׁנִית שְׂרִידֵינוּ. 85

בָּרַבִּים נִסֶּיךָ תַּרְאֵנוּ. 86

שָׁלוֹם תִּשְׁפּוֹת לָנוּ. 87

חֲמוֹל זְרוּיֶיךָ קְדוֹשֵׁנוּ. 88

וְרוּחַ נְדִיבָה תִסְמְכֵנוּ. 89

קוּמָה עֶזְרָתָה לָנוּ וּפְדֵנוּ. 90

אַל דֳּמִי לָךְ : 91

6 'THERE IS NONE LIKE YOU AMONG THE DUMB'
by Isaac bar Shalom

1 There is none like You among the dumb,
2 Keeping silence and being still in the face of those who
    aggrieve us.
3 Our foes are many; they rise up against us,
4 As they take counsel together to revile us.
5 'Where is your King?,' they taunt us.
6 But we have not forgotten You nor deceived You.
7   Do not keep silence!

8 Those driven from the midst of men became proud.
9 They crushed Your people with rigor.
10 Your enemies lifted up their head,
11 Those seekers of ghosts and of idols.
12 Our foes would judge us, and are saying:
13 'How now, you hapless Jews!'
14   Do not keep silence!

15 'Be receptive to advice,
16 Lest you turn into disgrace.
17 Yea, to quarrel and to strife.
18 But, if you will be like us,
19 Turning to us, coming close,
20 One people we shall be.'
21   Do not keep silence!

22 In answer cried the smitten ones:
23 'From our God we turn not, nor shall we worship yours!
24 "You shall utterly detest, and utterly abhor it."
25 Alive and enduring is our Redeemer,
26 Him we shall serve, and Him we praise.
27 In time of trouble, He is our salvation.'
28   Do not keep silence!

29 They made ready to slay their children,
30 Intending the blessing of sacrifice.
31 'Hear O Israel, the Lord is our God,
32 The Lord is One.' Let us proclaim His Unity!
33 For His Name's holiness are we slain,
34 Our wives and children are falling by the sword.
35   Do not keep silence!

36 As priests for the slaughter of their holocaust,
37 They bound the children and their mothers;
38 And, in the fire, they burned their skins,
39 Sprinkling the blood of sisters and brothers,
40 Offering as sweet savored sacrificial portions
41 The head and severed parts of flesh.
42   Do not keep silence!

43 A charred and overflowing pile,
44 Like an oven both uncovered and unswept;
45 All Israel weeps for the burning.
46 But those falling in God's fire
47 Are destined for His initiates' abode,

48 Like Hananiah, Mishael and Azariah.
49   Do not keep silence!

50 As refuse they treated Moses' Law,
51 The Talmud of Rabhina and Rabh Ashi.
52 Can You, at this, restrain Yourself and keep Your peace?
53 Pages and parchments destroyed by flailing sword,
54 Yet holy letters flying up on high—
55 God's writing on the tablets is engraved.
56   Do not keep silence!

57 The foe was strutting with his sword,
58 Destroyed my precious ones, made them to nought.
59 And he slew all who did my eye delight.
60 The year: four thousand nine hundred and seven,
61 When trouble closely followed trouble,
62 And, for my feet, they set a snare.
63   Do not keep silence!

64 The day when Nahshon hallowed God,
65 The foe struck at the apple of His eye;
66 On the twentieth day of the first month,
67 They were dashed to pieces, the expounders of weighty
68 And light matters of the Law, and of analogous reasoning,
69 Of statutes, ordinance and teachings.
70   Do not keep silence!

71 Almighty God, be zealous for Your Law.
72 Put on Your vengeance and Your zeal.
73 Arouse Your mighty power—
74 As You once rebuked the swinish beast
75 With destruction and havoc and breaking.
76 Him and his people You smote with the plague.
77   Do not keep silence!

78 Your right hand once smote the monster of the Nile.
79 Crush now with a hammer the skull of her

79

80 That sits securely, to her pleasures given.
81 Bright and ruddy as You came from Seir,
82 Scatter with destructive storm the one who now does rule.
83 Like a tested warrior, do arouse Your zeal!
84   Do not keep silence!

85 Make our remnants Your own once again.
86 Among crowds show us Your wonders.
87 Establish peace upon us!
88 Pity, O our Holy One, those whom You have dispersed;
89 Let a willing spirit uphold us.
90 Arise for our help, and redeem us!
91   Do not keep silence!

Commentary

The text of this poem may be found in *Siddur Otzar Hatephilloth*, Vilna, 1914, vol. 2, p. 256. Its listing in Davidson's *Thesaurus* is in vol. 1, p. 142, no. 3027. The poem is a *zulath*, i.e., a poem inserted in the benediction after the morning *Shema'* between the proclamation, 'There is no God beside You,' and the affirmation, 'You have been the help of our fathers from old.' See *Authorised Daily Prayer Book*, ed. Simeon Singer, p. 135. In the Ashkenazi rite, this poem is recited during the morning service of the first Sabbath after Passover. In that rite, the period between Passover and Pentecost is devoted to the commemoration of the Jewish communities in the Rhineland, martyred during the crusades. Its role as a *zulath*, in the section of the service celebrating God's redemptive acts, makes the message of the poem all the more poignant.

The poem consists of thirteen stanzas with a kind of irregular rhyme—usually two different rhymes in each stanza—and contains a complete alphabetical acrostic, followed by an acrostic of the poet's name, Isaac bar Shalom, and the wish, 'Be strong!'

Isaac bar Shalom lived in the twelfth century. See Zunz, *Literaturgeschichte der synagogalen Poesie*, Berlin, 1865, p. 458;

THE SILENT GOD

Eliezer Landshuth, *'Ammudé Ha-abhodah*, Berlin, 1857–62, p. 127. According to Landshuth, loc. cit., Isaac was describing the persecutions of the year 1147 in general, and the fate of one particular community which, however, is not further identified. The latter is evident from the specific date given in lines 60, 64, and 66, which together indicate the 20th day of Nissan, 4907 AM= 1147 CE.

During the second crusade (1147–9) many Jewish communities in France and Germany were destroyed. The usual procedure was for the Christian mob to confront the Jews with a choice between baptism and death. The Jews, on the whole, opted for the latter, and died 'for the sanctification of God's Name.' Lest their women and children fall into the hands of the mob, the Jewish men would kill them first—being themselves killed by the mob, if time did not permit them to fall by their own hand. The mob would then proceed to the burning of Torah Scrolls and the volumes of the Talmud.

Two motifs were uppermost in the minds of the Jews engaged in the act of 'sanctifying God's Name' with their lives. One was the 'Binding of Isaac,' described in Shalom Spiegel, *The Last Trial*, New York, 1967. The other was the sacrificial cult of biblical Israel, as in the poem under consideration here.

1 *There is none like You among the dumb.* This daring statement is based on Psalm 86:8, 'There is none like You among the gods, O Lord.' A similar statement is found in Exodus 15:11, 'Who is like You, O Lord, among the gods?' This latter verse was interpreted in the School of Rabbi Ishmael, with reference to the 'silence' of God at the time of the destruction of the Temple, as 'Who is like You, O Lord, among the dumb?', reading *illemim* (dumb) for the text's *elim* (gods). See b. *Gittin* 56b. The poet thus combines Psalm 86:8 with the Rabbinic comment on Exodus 15:11, in order to achieve the startling effect of his opening line.
7 *Do not keep silence!* A quotation from Psalm 83:2, used as a refrain throughout this poem.
8 *Those driven from the midst of men.* For this phrase, see Job 30:5.
24 *You shall utterly detest, etc.* A direct quotation from Deuteronomy

7:26, where it is used with reference to the cult of the Canaanites.
31-2 *Hear O Israel, etc.* The opening verse of the *Shema'*, Deuteronomy 6:4, the proclamation *par excellence* of Jewish monotheism. The Jewish martyrs would utter the *Shema'* at the point of death, to affirm the reason for their martyrdom.
36-41 The terminology of this stanza is that of the sacrificial legislation in the Book of Leviticus, where, of course, it refers to *animal* sacrifice.
44 *Like an oven both uncovered and unswept.* This is a concept discussed in connection with the Sabbath law, in *Tosephta Shabbath* II (III), 3, ed. Zuckermandel, p. 112. The poet borrows the terminology, not the law, for his own purpose.
45 *All Israel weeps for the burning.* A quotation from Leviticus 10:6.
48 *Like Hananiah, Mishael and Azariah.* The three young men who, according to Daniel, chapters 1-3, were thrown into the fiery furnace when they refused to pay homage to an idol. Unlike the martyrs of 1147, however, they survived their ordeal.
51 *The Talmud of Rabhina and Rabh Ashi.* According to tradition, though not necessarily according to the theories of modern scholarship, Rabhina and Rabh Ashi were the final redactors of the Babylonian Talmud. See Z. H. Chajes, *The Student's Guide through the Talmud*, London, 1952, p. 182.
54 *Yet holy letters flying up on high.* The phrase is based on b. 'Abhodah Zarah 18a, where the martyr's death of Rabbi Ḥanina b. Teradyon is described. He was burned alive while wrapped in a scroll of the Torah. His disciples asked him: 'Rabbi, what do you see?' He replied: 'The parchments are being burnt, but the letters are flying upward.'
55 *God's writing on the tablets is engraved.* See Exodus 32:16.
64 *The day when Nahshon hallowed God.* The Midrash (*Mekhilta, Beshallaḥ*, par. 5, ed. Horovitz-Rabin, pp. 105-7) tells that, while all the tribes were arguing about who would enter the Sea of Reeds first, Nahshon ben Amminadab, of the tribe of Judah, took the initiative and jumped into the sea first. God considered that to be an act of hallowing His Name, and, as a reward, the Davidic dynasty later arose out of the tribe of Judah. According to tradition, Israel's crossing of the Sea of Reeds took place on the

seventh day of Passover, which falls on 21st Nisan. Nahshon's jump into the sea must, therefore, be dated on the night following 20th Nisan, the date which the poet wants us to infer.

65 *the apple of His eye.* Deuteronomy 32:10 says that God keeps Israel 'as the apple of His eye.'

66 *On the twentieth day of the first month.* In line with Exodus 12:2, the month of Nisan is here reckoned as the first month of the year.

73 *Arouse Your mighty power.* A quotation from Psalm 80:3.

74 *the swinish beast.* Literally: 'The beast which roots with his snout like a swine.' See Eliezer ben Yehudah, *Thesaurus*, vol. 7, p. 3493, where this passage is quoted. In Psalm 80:14 the enemy is referred to as 'the boar out of the wood,' which Rashi takes to be a reference to Amalek. Amalek himself is a descendant of Esau-Edom, and 'Edom,' in Rabbinic and medieval Jewish literature, stands for Rome, both pagan and Christian.

78 *the monster of the Nile.* The Hebrew original has only the word *rahabh*, which refers to a mythical sea monster. However, passages like Psalm 87:4 make it clear that this is an emblematic name for Egypt; and, in Isaiah 30:7, *rahabh* is actually used as a parallel to Egypt. Our translation attempts to preserve the flavor of the original, while indicating its true meaning.

80 *That sits securely, to her pleasures given.* See Isaiah 47:8.

81 *Bright and ruddy as You came from Seir.* Literally: 'Bright and ruddy from Seir.' Seir = Edom; cf. Genesis 32:4. The poet combines two biblical passages. In Song of Songs 5:10, the young lover (identified with God in Rabbinic literature) is described as 'bright and ruddy.' In Isaiah 63:1-3, God is described as having red garments as He came from treading the winepress of Edom.

89 *Let a willing spirit uphold us.* A quotation from Psalm 51:14, turning the singular into a plural.

90 *Arise for our help, and redeem us.* See Psalm 44:27.

CHAPTER VIII

The Suffering God

The various reactions to adversity which we have discussed thus far are all based on the assumption that there is an almighty and all-powerful God who, for one reason or another, has decided to let His people undergo suffering and persecution. Such suffering and persecution may be accepted as just and deserved by the sufferers. Or, as some of the poems seem to indicate, they may give rise to a questioning of God's absolute justice, if not indeed to an outcry against God's intolerable silence.

But what if redemption is delayed, and if the exile is prolonged, because God Himself is, as it were, in exile and enslaved? What if, instead of conceiving of a punishing God and a suffering Israel, one were to think of God and Israel as fellow-sufferers, both in need of redemption?

Of course, such a thought must appear strange and far-fetched to modern Jews, brought up in the Maimonidean tradition which emphatically denies the applicability, in any literal sense, of anthropomorphism and anthropopathy to the Deity. Moreover, conditioned as he is by the need to define himself *vis à vis* Christianity, the modern Jew, particularly in the Western world, is liable to recoil from any suggestion that Judaism, too, knows about a 'suffering God.'

Yet the classical sources of Judaism, both biblical and Rabbinical, come to us from a period when the God of Israel had not yet been identified with the God of the philosophers, and when the legacies of Athens and Jerusalem had not yet been merged. Thus there is no *a priori* impossibility for such a concept to have arisen within Judaism; and there are enough passages in Rabbinic literature to show that there were Rabbis who did indeed espouse it. Even so, those Rabbis were well aware of the daring nature of such a thought, and they themselves gave utterance to it only because they believed that they had Scriptural warrant for doing so.

One of the key passages in the Bible which supplied the Rabbis with such a warrant is Isaiah 63:9. The way in which that verse is actually written would offer no support to any notion about a suffering God. It simply states: 'In all their troubles, no angel or messenger, His own Presence delivered them. In His love and pity He Himself redeemed them, raised them, and exalted them all the days of old.' That is the meaning we get from the Septuagint, the early Greek translation of the Bible, and that is the understanding of the text indicated in the marginal note of the new (1973) translation of the Book of Isaiah, issued by the Jewish Publication Society of America.

However, the *masorah*, the traditional version of the biblical text adopted for synagogue use, demands that one little word in that verse, the word *lo*, be read as though it were spelled with a *lamed* and a *waw*, and not as it is actually written in the text itself, with a *lamed* and an *aleph*. If, then, the text be read as the *masorah* wants us to read it, the entire meaning of the verse is changed. Instead of 'In all their troubles, no angel or messenger, His own Presence delivered them,' we now get: 'In all their troubles He was troubled, and the angel of His Presence delivered them.' Thus the main text of the new Jewish Publication Society version, which follows the *masorah*; and similarly already the 1917 translation of the Jewish Publication Society, which read: 'In all their affliction He was afflicted, and the angel of His presence saved them'—a translation which is identical with that of the Authorized Version which, in this instance, followed the *masorah*.

The Rabbis, not surprisingly, followed the reading presupposed by the *masorah*'s understanding of this text. Thus they quote Isaiah 63:9 by way of accounting for the fact that God revealed

Himself to Moses out of a thorn-bush, interpreting the verse as follows:[1]

> God said to Moses: 'Do you not feel that I live in pain just as the Israelites are living in pain? Know this from the place whence I am speaking to you, from out of the thorns. I am, as it were, a partner in their pain.'

The same Isaiah verse is also used in the following context:[2]

> You find that, every time Israel is enslaved, the *Shekhinah* (i.e., God's Presence), too, is, if one could say so, enslaved together with them. As it is said (Exodus 24:10): 'And they saw the God of Israel; and there was under His feet as it were a pavement of sapphire stone.' [The Hebrew, here translated as 'sapphire stone,' is *libhnath hassapir*, the word *libhnath* suggesting *lebhenah*= 'brick,' the symbol of Israel's slavery in Egypt.] But after they were redeemed, what does it say? 'Like the very heaven for clearness.' (ibid.) And it is said (Isaiah 63:9): 'In all their troubles He was troubled.'

If Isaiah 63:9 served the Rabbis as a proof text for the idea that God shared Israel's suffering and pain, it was Psalm 91:15 ('I will be with him in trouble') which suggested to them that God not only shared the afflictions of His people as a whole, but also the pain of every single individual.[3]

All such passages, and we have quoted only a sample of them, which speak of God's sharing Israel's afflictions, may, of course, indicate no more than that Israel, even in slavery, had an awareness of God's presence, and that God, in His mercy, made Himself accessible to suffering Israel—without, in any way, being Himself reduced in greatness and power. They may, on the other hand, also express more than that; and the frequent use in such passages of the term *kibheyakhol* ('as it were,' or 'if one could possibly say so') would tend to show that at least some of the Rabbis understood God's 'enslavement' as more real than symbolic.

Certainly this would seem to be the case with R. Aḥa's interpretation of Jeremiah 40:1. That verse reads: 'The word which came to Jeremiah from the Lord, after Nebuzaradan, the captain of the guard, had let him go from Ramah, when he had taken him being bound in chains among all the captives of Jerusalem and Judah that were carried away captive unto

Babylon.' R. Aḥa commented: 'If one could possibly say so, both
He [God] and he [Jeremiah] were bound in chains.'[4]

What R. Aḥa is saying is that the phrase, 'him being bound in
chains,' refers as much to God as it does to Jeremiah—a view
which could be justified on the basis of grammar and syntax
(viz: 'The word which came to Jeremiah from the Lord, after
Nebuzaradan . . . had taken Him bound in chains . . .'), even
though the plain meaning of the text would clearly make us infer
that the adverbial clause is connected with Jeremiah, and not with
the Lord. At any rate, the exegetical basis in Jeremiah 40:1 is
more transparent than it is in Ezekiel 1:1 ('as I was among the
captives'), which R. Aḥa cites as a parallel.[5]

Even more explicit about the effect of adversity upon God
Himself is a comment made by Rabbi Levi in the name of R.
Ḥama bar Ḥanina in connection with Exodus 17:16. That verse
occurs at the end of the report about Amalek's attack upon Israel
and Joshua's routing of Amalek. Moses, we are told, built an
altar, and called its name, 'The Lord is my banner.' The text goes
on to say: 'And he said: "The hand upon the throne of the Lord:
the Lord will have war with Amalek from generation to generation."' The Hebrew original, it should be pointed out, uses the
word kes for 'throne,' instead of the more usual kissé; and, for the
Lord's name, it has YH, instead of the more usual YHWH. That
is to say, both the 'throne' and the Lord's name appear here, as it
were, in an abbreviated form. Hence Rabbi Levi's comment:
'As long as the seed of Amalek exists in the world, neither God
nor His throne are complete. But, once the seed of Amalek has
disappeared from the world, then the throne will be complete,
and God will be complete.'[6]

Amalek, a descendant of Esau,[7] was not only the ancestor of
those who attacked Israel in the wilderness, but also, by Rabbinic
reckoning based on I Samuel 15:8 and Esther 3:1, the ancestor of
Haman in the Esther story. In Rabbinic literature, Amalek thus
becomes a cipher for evil in the world, for the arch-enemy of
Israel and, by implication, of God. What Rabbi Levi is saying,
therefore, is that, as long as Amalek holds sway in the world, as
long as evil has not been fully conquered, neither God nor His

sovereignty are complete. God, as it were, is limited. This notion of the incomplete God, of the God whose perfection has yet to be brought about, was to play a significant role in the sixteenth-century kabbalistic system of Isaac Luria.[8]

No less daring was Rabbi Akiba's comment on II Samuel 7:23. That text, as we shall amplify in our commentary on poem no. 7, presents a number of difficulties. Suffice it here to say that Rabbi Akiba understood the operative words to mean 'before Your people, whom You redeemed for Yourself from Egypt, the nation and its God.' Rabbi Akiba said: 'If it were not for the fact that Scripture itself explicitly states it, it would be impossible to say so. Israel, as it were, said to God: "You have redeemed Yourself!" '[9]

Eleazar Kallir, in the sixth century (?), not only takes Rabbi Akiba's interpretation of II Samuel 7:23 for granted, but he bases the whole of poem no. 7 on the idea that God, in saving Israel from Egypt, had actually saved Himself—even as Kallir uses several other Rabbinic passages which tell of God's sharing both Israel's sufferings and Israel's deliverances.

Henry Slonimsky has found in such ideas 'the philosophy implicit in the Midrash.'[10] He considers those ideas 'the boldest, most forward-reaching thought concerning God in the Midrash.'[11] This thought is that 'God depends on man for his strength and for his failure, for his growth and for his retrogression. In a world in which both are growing or in process, it is man who by his acts increases or decreases the stature of God.'[12]

Slonimsky is not unaware of the fact that both the Midrash and the liturgy contain many expressions to the effect that human guilt accounts for human suffering. But he regards those expressions as a 'magnificent and generous gesture of self-castigation which can be and has been misunderstood.' For him, 'the true view' is that suffering does indeed purify Israel from sins, but that Israel is also[13]

> the lamb or the dove on whom all evil and suffering must be tried out, because of some dread and ominous feature in the scheme of things whereby light can come only after all darkness, and goodness only after all evil has had its day, and where the elect must bear the

burden of the world by taking upon themselves all responsibility and all suffering.

It is arguable whether any of the Rabbis whom Slonimsky invokes would have owned up to a belief in an 'emergent God' whose destiny is so entirely dependent upon man, or whether Slonimsky was not reading back into the Rabbinic texts modernist theological notions about the finite or limited Deity which only gained currency in Slonimsky's own day.[14] It might be fair to say that the kind of Rabbinic expressions which we have encountered in this chapter do indeed lend themselves to the type of logical extension which Slonimsky assumes, but that, on the whole, the Rabbis themselves, unlike Slonimsky, did not fully pursue those logical implications.

In any case, Slonimsky is compelled to admit that the philosophy which he finds to be implicit in the Midrash is not the prevailing or predominant view of God in the Midrash.[15] One might go further than this. Not only is it impossible, in the face of evidence to the contrary, to saddle Rabbinic literature as a whole with a systematic theology which sees God as somehow limited and less than all-powerful, but it is even doubtful whether those Rabbis who, on occasion, ventured the suggestion about God's present limitations were themselves consistent in viewing God in that manner under all circumstances.

This is something which will have to be borne in mind also in connection with the poems discussed in this and in previous chapters. Adversity may wring from the human heart the kind of outcry which, in more settled moments, would be considered outside the boundaries of normative theology. Neither Rabbis nor poets are necessarily consistent in matters of the spirit. As Solomon Schechter has pointed out, 'whatever the faults of the Rabbis were, consistency was not one of them.'[16] This was necessarily so, because 'with God as a reality, Revelation as a fact, Torah as a rule of life, and the hope of Redemption as a most vivid expectation, they felt no need for formulating their dogmas into a creed . . . What they had of theology, they enunciated spasmodically or "by impulses." '[17]

Similarly, it would be a mistake to assume that Judah Halevi's

relation to God was dominated by the thought that Israel's
'claim' on God was as justified as Tamar's on Judah, or that Isaac
bar Shalom knew God only as the One who remains silent in the
face of Israel's sufferings. It is enough to be aware of the existence
of certain 'daring' and unconventional thoughts in Rabbinic
literature, and of their availability to such medieval poets who,
with all of their own daring and unconventionality, nevertheless
utilized them for an enrichment of the traditional liturgy.

It is different with the Lurianic Kabbalah of the sixteenth
century, which clearly incorporated some of those 'daring' ideas
into a consistent theological system. Nor would we rule out the
possibility that, by way of a religious response to the Holocaust
of our time, some of those ideas may yet constitute important
ingredients for the various formulations of a modern Jewish
theology.

This much, though, is certain: that the doctrine of 'on account
of our sins' is neither the last word spoken in the face of adversity,
nor was it, even in the Rabbinic period itself, the only theological
option available to the teachers of Judaism.

כהושעת אלים בלוד

מאת ר' אלעזר הקליר

אֲנִי וָהוֹ הוֹשִׁיעָה נָּא :

כְּהוֹשַׁעְתָּ אֵלִים בְּלוּד עִמָּךְ. 1
בְּצֵאתְךָ לְיֵשַׁע עַמָּךְ. 2
כֵּן הוֹשַׁעְנָא : 3

כְּהוֹשַׁעְתָּ גּוֹי וֵאלֹהִים. 4
דְּרוּשִׁים לְיֵשַׁע אֱלֹהִים. 5
כֵּן הוֹשַׁעְנָא : 6

7 כְּהוֹשַׁעְתָּ הֲמוֹן צְבָאוֹת.

8 וְעִמָּם מַלְאֲכֵי צְבָאוֹת.

9 כֵּן הוֹשַׁעְנָא:

10 כְּהוֹשַׁעְתָּ זַכִּים מִבֵּית עֲבָדִים.

11 חַנּוּן בְּיָדָם מַעֲבִידִים.

12 כֵּן הוֹשַׁעְנָא:

13 כְּהוֹשַׁעְתָּ טְבוּעִים בְּצוּל גְּזָרִים.

14 יְקָרְךָ עִמָּם מַעֲבִירִים.

15 כֵּן הוֹשַׁעְנָא:

16 כְּהוֹשַׁעְתָּ כַּנָּה מְשׁוֹרֶרֶת וַיּוֹשַׁע.

17 לְגוֹחָהּ מְצֻיֶּנֶת וַיִּוָּשַׁע.

18 כֵּן הוֹשַׁעְנָא:

19 כְּהוֹשַׁעְתָּ מַאֲמַר וְהוֹצֵאתִי אֶתְכֶם.

20 נָקוּב וְהוֹצֵאתִי אִתְּכֶם.

21 כֵּן הוֹשַׁעְנָא:

22 כְּהוֹשַׁעְתָּ סוֹבְבֵי מִזְבֵּחַ.

23 עוֹמְסֵי עֲרָבָה לְהַקִּיף מִזְבֵּחַ.

24 כֵּן הוֹשַׁעְנָא:

25 כְּהוֹשַׁעְתָּ פִּלְאֵי אָרוֹן כְּהָפְשַׁע.

26 צַעַר פְּלֶשֶׁת בַּחֲרוֹן אַף וְנוֹשַׁע.

27 כֵּן הוֹשַׁעְנָא:

28 כְּהוֹשַׁעְתָּ קְהִלּוֹת בָּבֶלָה שִׁלַּחְתָּ.

29 רַחוּם לְמַעֲנָם שִׁלַּחְתָּ.

30 כֵּן הוֹשַׁעְנָא:

כְּהוֹשַׁעְתָּ שְׁבוּת שִׁבְטֵי יַעֲקֹב. 31
תָּשׁוּב וְתָשִׁיב שְׁבוּת אָהֳלֵי יַעֲקֹב. 32
וְהוֹשִׁיעָה נָּא: 33

אֲנִי וָהוֹ הוֹשִׁיעָה נָּא:

7 'GOD, SAVE YOURSELF AND US!'
by Eleazar Kallir

'*Ani Waho*, save now!'

1 As You saved Israel in Egypt, together with Yourself,
2 When You went forth to save Your people,
3   So save now.

4 As You have saved the nation and its God,
5 Sought out for God's salvation,
6   So save now.

7 As You have saved the multitudinous hosts,
8 And with them the angelic hosts,
9   So save now.

10 As You have saved the pure ones from the house of bondage,
11 O Gracious One, as You saved those enslaved with manual
    labor,
12   So save now.

13 As You saved those about to drown in the deep divided sea,
14 Who made Your own glory pass through the sea with them,
15   So save now.

16 As You have saved the stock which sang: 'And He saved,'
17 Distinguished by its Deliverer so that He Himself was saved,
18   So save now.

19 As You have saved by uttering: 'And I will bring you out,'
20 Which is explained: 'With you, I shall be brought out,'
21   So save now.

22 As You have saved those circling 'round the altar,
23 Carrying the willow to surround the altar,
24   So save now.

25 As You have saved the Ark with wonders when it was torn away,
26 Causing pain to Philistia in anger, and it was saved,
27   So save now.

28 As You have saved the congregation You sent to Babylon,
29 For their sake, God of mercy, Yourself You were sent there,
30   So save now.

31 As You have saved the captive tribes of Jacob,
32 Restore again the captive tents of Jacob,
33   And save now.

      '*Ani Waho*, save now!'

Commentary

The text of this poem may be found in Arthur Davis and Herbert M. Adler, eds, *Service of the Synagogue*, Tabernacles volume, 14th ed., London, 1949, pp. 144–5. Its listing in Davidson's *Thesaurus* is in vol. 2, pp. 466ff., no. 110. The poem is a *hosha'nah*, that is to say, a liturgical poem recited during the circumambulations of the reading desk in the synagogue, when the worshippers carry the Tabernacles festival bouquet. The poem contains a complete alphabetical acrostic, and each stanza has its own primitive rhyme —often achieved by the repetition of the same word at the end of the lines. There is no meter. The author is Eleazar Kallir, who may have lived in Palestine, in the sixth century. See about him in *Encyclopaedia Judaica*, vol. 10, cols 713–15.

The key to the understanding of this poem is provided by the exclamation with which it begins and ends: *ani waho hoshi'ah na.* It is found in *Mishnah Sukkah* 4:5, within the following context:

> Each day [of the Feast of Tabernacles] they went in procession around the altar once, and said: 'Save now, O Lord, we beseech You! Send now prosperity, O Lord, we beseech You!' (Psalm 118:25.) Rabbi Judah said: '*Ani waho*, save now!' But on that day [i.e., on the seventh day of Tabernacles] they went in procession around the altar seven times.

The phrase *ani waho* has been variously interpreted. It has been pointed out, for example, that the numerical value of the Hebrew letters of *ani waho* is identical with the numerical value of the Hebrew letters of 'O Lord, we beseech You.' Rabbi Judah, therefore, thought of the people taking part in the procession as avoiding the pronunciation of the Divine Name—just as that pronunciation was avoided in the Rabbinic period.

On the other hand, the phrase also lends itself to the translation: 'I and He'—in which case the meaning of *ani waho hoshi'ah na* would be that God should save Himself as well as the worshipper. It is in this latter sense that Rabbenu Hai Gaon (939–1038) interpreted the phrase. See Chaim M. Horowitz, ed., *Torathan shel rishonim*, vol. 1, Frankfurt aM, 1881, p. 51; and B. M. Lewin, ed., *Otzar Hageonim*, vol. 6, part 2, Jerusalem, 1934, p. 66. Hai's father, Sherira, is credited by Judah b. Bile'am (*ca.* 1070–1100) with the same interpretation. See Albert Harkavy, ed., *Hadashim gam yeshanim*, no. 7, Warsaw, 1895–6, p. 22.

The same interpretation is given by, among others, the *Tosaphoth* to b. *Sukkah* 45a, *s.v. ani waho*; and it has actually been 'codified' in *Tur, Orah Hayyim, Hilkhoth Lulabh* no. 660, and *Beth Yoseph*, ad loc.

See also Schalom Ben-Chorin, ' "Ich und Er": eine Liturgische Formel,' *Zeitschrift für Religions- und Geistesgeschichte*, 11 (1959), pp. 267–9.

There can be no doubt that, whatever the original meaning of *ani waho* may have been in the Mishnah, our poet understood the phrase to mean: 'I and He'—in the sense that, by saving Israel,

God saves Himself. Eight of the eleven stanzas express this theme clearly and explicitly; others possibly hint at it.

1 *Israel.* This is commonly taken to be the meaning of the Hebrew word *elim* in this stanza. The literal translation is 'mighty ones.' A better derivation would be from *elim*= 'terebinths,' as in Isaiah 61:3, where it is said of *Israel* that 'they shall be called terebinths of righteousness.' However, Heidenheim, in his commentary on this poem, identifies *elim* with 'angels,' an identification which, in the case of the synonymous *elohim*, is quite common in Rabbinic literature. Since angels are understood as a manifestation of God, the poet would, if Heidenheim is correct, sound his major theme already at the very beginning of the poem; and the first stanza would have to be rendered: 'As You saved angels together with Yourself in Egypt, when You went forth to save Your people, so save now.' Heidenheim's interpretation is, in our view, somewhat doubtful, if only because the 'together with Yourself' makes the mention of angels in this stanza unnecessary in terms of the poet's scheme; and we prefer to see in *elim* a reference to Israel.

Egypt. The Hebrew text has *Lud*, which must here be understood in the light of Genesis 10:13, 'And Mizraim begot Ludim.' *Mizraim* is, of course, the Hebrew word for Egypt.

4 *the nation and its God.* This is based on the difficult verse, II Samuel 7:23, which concludes with the words, 'before Your people, whom You redeemed for Yourself from Egypt, nations and its gods.' See Abraham Geiger, *Hamiqra wethargumaw*, Jerusalem, 1949, pp. 186ff., and Arnold B. Ehrlich, *Miqra kipheshuto*, 2nd ed., New York, 1969, vol. 2, p. 203. And see George A. Buttrick *et al.*, eds, *The Interpreter's Bible*, vol. 2, New York and Nashville, 1953, pp. 1086–8. The traditional Jewish exegesis, as reflected, for example, by Kimḥi and Altschuler ad loc., understands the last phrase in the sense of God's having redeemed His people *from* nations and their gods. Indeed, in its translation of this text, even the AV inserts the word, 'from.' Our poet, by way of contrast, takes the Hebrew text literally as it stands, and reads into the text the meaning that, through the

Exodus from Egypt, God redeemed a nation (= Israel) and its God (= Himself). Kallir was preceded in this by Rabbi Akiba, who is reported to have said in connection with this text: 'If it were not for the fact that Scripture itself explicitly states it, it would be impossible to say so. Israel, as it were, said to God: "You have redeemed Yourself!"' See *Mekhilta, Masekheth dePisha*, ch. 14, ed. Horovitz-Rabin, p. 51; *Siphré, Beha'alothekha, pisqa* 84, ed. Friedmann, p. 22b; *Yalqut Shime'oni*, II Samuel, no. 146.

7 *the multitudinous hosts.* Israel. Cf. Exodus 12:41.

8 *the angelic hosts.* The Midrash (*Exodus Rabbah* 33:4) sees in Psalm 68:13, which it applies to the angels, a parallel to Exodus 12:41. This leads to the thought that, when Israel left Egypt, they were accompanied by angels. Yet, according to *Exodus Rabbah* 32:4, 'the angels are sustained only by the splendor of the *Shekhinah*,' i.e., the angels are, as it were, a kind of extension of the Deity. When, therefore, in saving Israel, God likewise saved the angels, He thus also saved an aspect of Himself.

11 *O Gracious One, etc.* A difficult clause. The words, 'as You saved those,' are not in the Hebrew text, but have been inserted to indicate what we believe to be the meaning of that text. Another, and somewhat more daring, interpretation might be: 'They [i.e., the Egyptians] with their hand [= their power] were enslaving the Gracious One.' This might be more in line with the over-all scheme of this poem, which makes God's self-redemption parallel His redemption of Israel. But the syntactical construction of this stanza would then be even more difficult.

16 *the stock.* A synonym for Israel, based on Psalm 80:15, where Israel is described as 'the stock which Your right hand has planted.'

'*And He saved.*' The opening word of Exodus 14:30. The reference is actually to the Song of the Reed Sea, Exodus, chapter 15. But, in the liturgy of the Synagogue, Exodus 15 is always introduced by Exodus 14:30-1. See *Authorised Daily Prayer Book*, pp. 34ff.

17 *He Himself was saved.* The word for 'And He saved,' *wayyosha'*, in Exodus 14:30, can, with an alteration of the vocalization only, be read as *wayyiwwasha'* ('and He was saved'). This reading, implying that God was saved when Israel was saved, had been suggested as a homiletical possibility by Rabbi Meir (second century CE). Cf. *Tanḥuma, Aḥaré,* ed. Buber, pp. 34b and 36a; see also *Numbers Rabbah* 2:2.

19 *'And I will bring you out.'* The first of the four 'promises of redemption' in Exodus 6:6–7.

20 *'With you, I shall be brought out.'* As in the case of the first word of Exodus 14:30, which, by a change in vocalization, can be read as 'and He was saved,' so, in Exodus 6:6, the words *wehotzethi ethkhem* ('and I shall bring you out') can, by a change in vocalization, yield the reading *wehutzethi ittekhem* ('and I shall be brought out with you'). While the thought itself, as we have already seen, is not unknown in Rabbinic literature, this particular treatment of the words in Exodus 6:6 seems to be original with Kallir in this poem; for it is this very stanza which is quoted by M. M. Kasher in his *Torah Shelemah,* vol. 9, New York, 1945, p. 10, as the source of this interpretation.

23 *Carrying the willow.* Cf. *Mishnah Sukkah* 4:5, for the custom of surrounding the altar with willows on the Feast of Tabernacles.

25–6 *As You have saved the Ark,* etc. The reference is to the story about the capture of the Ark of the Covenant by the Philistines, God's punishment of the Philistines, and the eventual return of the Ark to the Israelites, in I Samuel, chapters 5 and 6. Since the Ark was thought of as a kind of 'throne' for God, His saving of the Ark is related to the theme of God's saving of Himself.

28 *You sent to Babylon.* A reference to the Babylonian Exile, making use of the words in Isaiah 43:14, 'for your sake I have sent to Babylon.'

29 *Yourself You were sent there.* By changing the vocalization of *shillaḥti* ('I sent'), in Isaiah 43:14, to *shullaḥti,* one obtains the meaning of 'I was sent.' This seems to be implied already by the context in which Isaiah 43:14 is quoted in b. *Megillah* 29a. In *Mekhilta, Masekheth de Pisḥa,* ch. 14, ed. Horovitz-Rabin, p. 52, and in *Leviticus Rabbah* 32:8, the verse is actually quoted as though the text, in fact, read: 'for your sake I was sent to Babylon.' Cf. also Jedidiah Norzi (sixteenth–seventeenth centuries), who refers at length to our poem in his commentary, *Minḥath Shai,* to Isaiah 43:13.

CHAPTER IX

A Somber View of Man

It is unlikely that, in an earlier age, a book focusing primarily, though not exclusively, on synagogal poetry of a somewhat unconventional or unusual theological character would have included poem no. 8. It is a poem which speaks of man's being prone to sin, of his physical weakness, and of his great difficulty in meeting the standards set by God. The only life our poet finds meaningful is the life lived in obedience to God's will. The poem is, therefore, an eloquent exemplification of what Erich Fromm has called 'authoritarian religion,' defined by him as 'the surrender to a power transcending man. The main virtue of this type of religion is obedience, its cardinal sin is disobedience. Just as the deity is conceived as omnipotent and omniscient, man is conceived as being powerless and insignificant.'[1]

There were times when the burden of this poem would not have been felt to be unusual or out of keeping with the normative theological position of Judaism. But times have changed. Abraham Geiger, in 1870, still found it possible to include this poem in his Day of Atonement liturgy.[2] So did the 'union prayerbook' (*Einheitsgebetbuch*) of German Liberal Judaism, in 1929.[3] And, for that matter, so did the 1945 revision of the ritual of American Reform Judaism.[4] But it is missing in the Reconstructionist *High Holiday Prayer Book* of 1948; nor is it contained in *Gate of Repentance*, the prayerbook published in 1973 by the Union of Liberal and Progressive Synagogues in London, which has been adopted as the basis for the next revision of the American Reform Jewish prayerbook. Even the new American Conservative *Maḥzor for Rosh Hashanah and Yom Kippur*, edited by Jules Harlow, and published by the Rabbinical Assembly in 1972, omits this poem.

The fate of the poem may, in part, be due to the upsurge in our time of what Erich Fromm calls 'humanistic religion,' which 'is centered around man and his strength ... Man's aim in humanistic religion is to achieve the greatest strength, not the greatest power-lessness; virtue is self-realization, not obedience ... Inasmuch as humanistic religions are theistic, God is a symbol of *man's own powers* which he tries to realize in his life, and not a symbol of force and domination, *having power over man*.'[5]

It has become fashionable in our time, even among some Jews who think of themselves as religious, to follow Erich Fromm not only in his classification of the two types of religion, but also in the value judgments he passed by condemning 'authoritarian religion' and commending the 'humanistic' variety. Recent efforts of liturgical reform in Judaism point in that direction.

But the desire to glory in human achievement, to reject man's self-abasement before God, and to celebrate his creative capacities, did not have to wait for Erich Fromm's definitions and value judgments. The eighteenth and nineteenth centuries already bequeathed to us a concept of man and an estimation of man's rationality and capacity for unlimited progress, which, if anything, had to be modified rather than enhanced by twentieth-century psychological insight and historical reality. Yet it was precisely in the nineteenth century that the great new systems of Jewish theology were created, and that the Jewish pulpits echoed with the glorification of man as 'God's partner in the work of Creation.'

Neither the phrase nor the concept was altogether new. As early as the second century CE, Rabbi Akiba had indicated that, while God does indeed furnish the raw materials, it was man who succeeded in making the best use of them. He substantiated that assertion by comparing raw ears of corn with delicate white bread, and bundles of wet flax with 'garments made in Beth Shean.'[6] And 'all our Rabbis, in the name of Rabbi Ḥanina,'

noting that the same Hebrew letters—though in different arrange-
ments—spell the word 'very' (*me-od*) and the word 'man'
(*adam*), concluded that Genesis 1:31, 'God saw everything He had
made, and, behold, it was very (*me-od*) good', really meant:
'Behold, man (*adam*) is good!'[7] Rabbi Abin Halevi declared:
'There are four exalted ones in the world: The most exalted
among the beasts is the lion. The most exalted among the animals
is the ox. The most exalted among the birds is the eagle. But man
is exalted above them all.'[8]

Still, when it came to calling man 'God's partner in the work of
Creation,' the ancient Rabbis were somewhat more sparing in the
use of that appellation than were their successors in the nineteenth
and twentieth centuries. They seem to have used it, in fact, only
in connection with two specific human activities. One was the
rendering of 'a true judgment according to its truth' by a human
judge.[9] The other was the Jew's recitation of Genesis 2:1-3 as
part of the prayer on Sabbath Eve—which implied man's testimony to the Creator role of God.[10]

If the ancient Rabbis were somewhat less exuberant than their
latter-day successors in the glorification of man, it may be that
they had a somewhat greater awareness of the fact that the Bible,
which in Psalm 8:6 tells us that God had made man 'but little
lower than the angels,' also contains such books as Ecclesiastes and
Job. At any rate, the literature of the Rabbis presents us with a
rather more balanced view of the human condition.[11]

Even more at variance with what, in modern times, has
generally been proclaimed as *the* 'Jewish view of man,' is the
following passage in the Talmud, recording a famous debate of
the early Rabbinic period:[12]

> Our Rabbis taught: For two and a half years the School of Shammai
> disputed with the School of Hillel. The former said that it would
> have been better for man not to have been created than to have been
> created. The latter said that it was better for man to have been
> created than not to have been created.
>
> They finally voted and decided that it would indeed have been
> better for man not to have been created than to have been created.
> But now that he has, in fact, been created, let man examine his past
> deeds. Others say: Let him scrutinize his future actions.

What makes this passage so particularly remarkable is the
Rabbis' general reluctance to bring theological opinions to a vote.
Theological views were, as a rule, simply recorded in all of their
diversity, without any attempt being made to determine the
opinion of the majority. Indeed, as Leo Baeck remarked, 'this
sentence which would make pessimism a doctrine of the faith . . .
meets an essential presupposition of dogma.'[13]

But Baeck, who denied the existence of dogmas in Judaism,
also underlines the fact that, in spite of its quasi-dogmatic formulation, the decision that 'it would have been better if man had not
been created' never did attain to a position of dogma in Judaism,
and had never been considered as such. Indeed, Ephraim E.
Urbach has attempted to show that the decision reached by the
two schools must not be taken at face value, and that, at most,
the topic of the debate was 'the wicked man,' rather than man
as such.[14]

Be that as it may. The fact remains that Rabbinic literature, as
a whole, was not given to any unqualified glorification of man,
and that, contrary to much of modern Jewish apologetics, the
ancient Rabbis by no means regarded the emphasis on man's
proneness to sin as a monopoly of Christianity. What is more, the
somber view of man became enshrined in the liturgy.

A prayer, originally meant for the Day of Atonement,[15] but
included in the daily liturgy at least since the first Jewish prayerbook, the ninth-century *Seder Rabh 'Amram Gaon*, describes the
human condition in the following terms:[16]

Master of all the worlds!
Not because of our righteousness do we lay our
supplications before You,
But because of Your abundant mercies.
For what are we?
What is our life?
What is our piety?
What is our righteousness?
What our help?
What our strength?
What our might?
What can we say before You, O Lord our God
and God of our fathers?

Are not the mightiest men as nought before You?
The men of renown as though they had never been?
The wisest as if without knowledge?
And the men of understanding as if without intelligence?
For so much of their doing is confusion;
And the days of their lives are as vanity before You.
Man's advantage over the beast is nought,
For all is vanity.

The prayer does indeed go on to say that, because of God's covenant with the patriarchs, there is meaning and joy in the life of faith, so that, apparently, the 'vanity' of human existence can be transcended. But the 'vanity' itself is not overlooked; nor is Ecclesiastes' conclusion (3:19) that 'man's advantage over the beast is nought.'

That latter theme also finds expression in a meditative poem by Solomon Ibn Gabirol (ca. 1020–ca. 1057), of which the opening lines read as follows:[17]

You dwellers in bodies of clay,
Why lift up your eyes and be gay,
When every advantage you thought
To have over beasts is but nought?

Gabirol's poem is a *tokheḥah* (literally: 'reproof'), a type of moralistic poem, developing the theme of human weakness and finitude, and urging man to repent. Gabirol has left us several poems of this kind. This is all the more noteworthy in view of the fact that the Spanish Jewry within which Gabirol had his being was one not at all adverse to the pleasures of life—living as they did under political circumstances which made those enjoyments possible. Gabirol himself was the author of secular love- and drinking-songs.[18]

Man's finitude and the vanity of mundane existence are themes to which medieval Jewish poets revert time and again, developing insights already stated clearly in both Bible and Rabbinic literature. The Mishnah, for example, records the following advice, given by Rabbi Levitas of Jabneh: 'Be exceedingly humble of spirit, for all that man can hope for is the worm.'[19] Rabbi Eleazar Hakkappar is quoted as saying:[20]

Against your will you were fashioned, and against your will you were born. Against your will you live, and against your will you die. Against your will you are destined to give an account of yourself before the King of kings, the Holy One, praised be He.

In this connection, it should be borne in mind that, for Rabbinic and medieval Judaism, man was really finite, and death was very real. There was, of course, the belief and hope in resurrection and immortality. But immortality was not automatic. It was not a part of Rabbinic anthropology—as though man were, by definition, an immortal creature. Rather was immortality considered under the heading of 'Divine Retribution' or 'Reward and Punishment.' If man wanted to have a share in the World-to-Come, he had to earn and deserve that share—through obedience to God's Law and, as Maimonides would put it, through holding the correct kind of metaphysical views. That is the reason why, in the *tokheḥah* poems, a contemplation of man's finitude serves as a prelude to the call for repentance.

It is in that tradition that poem no. 8 was composed. Strange, therefore, as that poem might seem to the modern Jew, reared in a modernist faith of nineteenth-century vintage, within its own medieval setting the poem merely expressed an evaluation of the human condition which was quite generally accepted.

We do not know who its author was, or when and where he lived. It has occasionally been attributed to Meshullam ben Kalonymos of the tenth and eleventh centuries.[21] But the experts in this field, beginning with Leopold Zunz and Eliezer Landshuth in the last century, have denied Meshullam's authorship—without, however, being able to name another author in his place.[22] S. D. Luzzatto even surmised that our poem was one of the most ancient pieces of synagogal poetry, and that it was composed in Asia. But he offered no proof for his surmise.[23]

The fact that neither the time nor the place of the poem's origin can be properly determined again underlines the general acceptance of the somber view of man which it expresses. Yet it would be wrong to see in this poem the end-all and be-all of what medieval Judaism had to say on the subject of man. The poem reflects one aspect of the human condition. There are others; and medieval Judaism was aware of them, too. Its total approach to the subject can perhaps be summarized best by something which a post-medieval Rabbi, Simḥah Bunam of Pzhysha (d. 1827), once said to his disciples:[24]

Everyone must have two pockets, so that he can reach into the one or the other, according to his needs. In his right pocket are to be the words: 'For my sake was the world created,' and in his left: 'I am dust and ashes.'

אנוש מה יזכה

מאת מחבר עלום השם

1   אֱנוֹשׁ מַה יִזְכֶּה
וּצְבָא דַק לֹא זַכּוּ בְּעֵינֶיךָ:

2   בַּלָּחִים אִם תִּבְעַר הָאֵשׁ
מַה בֶּחָצִיר יָבֵשׁ:

3   גָּלוּי לְךָ חֹשֶׁךְ כְּמוֹ אוֹר
מְשׁוֹטֵט כֹּל בְּעָיִן:

4   דִּירָתְךָ בַּסֵּתֶר
וּגְלוּיוֹת לְךָ כָּל־נִסְתָּרוֹת:

5   הַדָּן יְחִידִי
וְהוּא בְאֶחָד וּמִי יְשִׁיבֶנּוּ:

6   וְעַל גּוֹי וְעַל אָדָם יַחַד יִנְטֶה קַו
וְאֵין מִי יַרְשִׁיעַ:

7   זֹאת יָבִין כָּל־יְצִיר
וְלֹא יַתְעוֹ יֵצֶר לַחֲטוֹא לְיוֹצֵר:

8 חֻתְּלַת בְּאֵרוֹ חֲפִירַת בּוֹרוֹ
חֶשְׁבּוֹן בּוֹרְאוֹ:

9 טָמֵא מִשְּׁאֵרוֹ וּמְטַמֵּא בְּעוֹדוֹ
וּמְטַמֵּא בְּמוֹתוֹ:

10 יְמֵי חַיָּיו תֹּהוּ וְלֵילוֹתָיו בֹּהוּ
וְעִנְיָנָיו הָבֶל:

11 כַּחֲלוֹם מֵהָקִיץ נִדְמָה
בַּלָּהוֹת יְבַעֲתוּהוּ תָמִיד:

12 לַיְלָה לֹא יִשְׁכַּב יוֹמָם לֹא יָנוּחַ
עַד יֵרָדַם בַּקֶּבֶר:

13 מַה יִּתְאוֹנֵן אָדָם חַי
דַּיּוֹ אֲשֶׁר הוּא חָי:

14 נוֹלָד לְעָמָל וִיגִיעָה
אַשְׁרָיו אִם יְהִי יְגִיעוֹ בְּדַת אֱמֶת:

15 סוֹפוֹ עַל רֹאשׁוֹ מוֹכִיחַ
וְלָמָּה יַחֲנִיף:

16 עוֹד חֹתָמוֹ מְעִידוֹ עַל פָּעֳלוֹ
וּמַה יִּגְנֹב דָּעַת:

17 פּוֹעֵל צְדָקוֹת אִם יְהִי
יְלַוּוּהוּ לְבֵית עוֹלָמוֹ:

18 צוֹפֶה בְחָכְמָה אִם יְהִי
עִמּוֹ תִּתְלוֹנֵן בְּכֵלְחוֹ:

19 קָצוּף בְּדָמִים וּבְמִרְמָה אִם יְהִי
חֲרוּצִים יָמָיו:

20 רְצוֹנוֹ וְחֶפְצוֹ בִּהְיוֹת בְּמוּסָר
יָנוּב בְּשֵׂיבָה טוֹבָה:

21 שֵׁם טוֹב אִם יִקְנֶה
מִשְּׂמוֹת נְעִימִים אֲשֶׁר יִקָּרֵא:

22 תַּחַת כֵּן
יוֹם הַמִּיתָה מִיּוֹם לֵידָה הוּטָב:

8 'HOW CAN MAN BE PURE?'
author unknown

1 How can man be pure,
   if heaven's hosts are impure in Your sight?

2 If fire burns the verdant trees,
   what chance for withered grass?

3 Darkness is clear to You as light,
   who, with Your eye, survey all things.

4 Though hidden is Your dwelling-place,
   all secrets are revealed to You.

5 You judge as solitary Judge;
   and, being One, none contradicts.

6 Over men and nations You stretch out the line;
   there is none to fault You.

7 Let every creature heed this,
   lest impulse will seduce him to sin against his Creator:

8 The swaddling at his birth, the digging of his grave,
    the account due his Maker!

9 Impure from his flesh, defiled while still alive,
    man defiles others at his death.

10 Empty are his living days, void are his nights;
    and his pursuits are vanity.

11 He is like a dream when one awakes;
    terrors affright him all the time.

12 By night he cannot sleep, by day he cannot rest—
    until he slumbers in the grave.

13 But why should living man complain?
    Enough for him to be alive!

14 Born to trouble and to toil,
    he should be happy to toil in the Law of Truth.

15 His end gives proof of his beginning;
    why, then, his flattery?

16 At last his seal attests his work;
    what use, then, his deceit?

17 If man does acts of righteousness,
    they follow him to his eternal home.

18 If in wisdom he be circumspect,
    it dwells with him in hoary age.

19 If he brings wrath through murder and deceit,
    his days are prematurely cut.

20 If virtue be his striving and delight,
    he will bear fruit in ripe old age.

21 If he acquires a good name,
　　　far better 'tis than what he's called.

22 This being so,
　　　the day of death is better than the day of birth.

Commentary

The text of this poem may be found in Arthur Davis and Herbert
M. Adler, eds, *Service of the Synagogue*, Day of Atonement volume,
part 2, 14th ed., London, 1949, p. 56. Its listing in Davidson's
Thesaurus is in vol. 1, p. 295, no. 6476. The poem has a complete
alphabetical acrostic, but neither meter nor rhyme—except in
stanzas 7, 8, and 9 where the poet's 'punning' results in a natural
kind of rhyme, and in stanzas 13 and 21 where a rhyme seems to
have been intended.

The somber view of man, reflected in this poem, is somewhat
relieved by the setting in which it is placed by the Ashkenazi rite
in the morning service of the Day of Atonement. There it is
inserted, in the reader's repetition of the *'Amidah*, in the benediction which deals with the Resurrection. Both before the
beginning and after the end of this poem, the affirmation is made:
'Until the day of a man's death You wait for him to do repentance, so that You may turn him to revival.' Cf. Ezekiel 33:11.

1 *How can man be pure, etc?* For the thought, see Job 15:14ff. The
word 'pure,' in the language of the courts, and that is the sense
intended here, means 'just,' 'innocent.' See Jacob Levy, *Wörterbuch*,
vol. 1, p. 535.
5 *You judge as solitary Judge.* To human judges, on the other hand,
Rabbi Ishmael gave the advice: 'Judge not alone, for none may
judge alone save One.' (*Mishnah Aboth* 4:8.) In referring to God
as the solitary Judge, the poet uses the terminology of Rabbi
Ishmael's statement.

being One, none contradicts. Cf. Job 23:13.
7 In the Hebrew original, this stanza achieves its effect by means

of a multiple pun. The words here translated as 'creature,'
'impulse,' and 'Creator,' are all derived from the same Hebrew
root and have a similarity of sound, viz.: *yetzir, yetzer, yotzer.*
About the 'impulse,' here used in the sense of 'evil impulse,' see
Frank C. Porter, 'The Yeçer Hara,' in *Biblical and Semitic Studies*
by the Members of the Semitic and Biblical Faculty of Yale
University, New York, 1901, pp. 93–156.

8 Here, too, the poet's artistry lies partly in a multiple pun, the
words translated as 'his birth' (literally: 'his well'), 'his grave,' and
'his Maker,' all having a similar sound in Hebrew, viz.: *be-ero, boro,
bore-o.* The thought itself goes back to Akabya ben Mahalaleel,
who said: 'Consider three things, and you will not come into the
power of sin: Know whence you came, and whither you are
going, and before whom you are destined to give an account and
reckoning.' (*Mishnah Aboth* 3:1.)

9 *Impure from his flesh, etc.* According to biblical law (Leviticus,
chapters 12–15), greatly elaborated by the Rabbis, there are any
number of normal and abnormal physical conditions which can
render a person ritually impure. At the same time, as long as a
person is alive, he is liable to become ritually defiled through the
levitical impurities of others; while, at the moment of his death,
those who come in contact with his body, or find themselves
under the same roof with it, are rendered levitically impure.

16 *At last his seal attests his work.* Based on the Rabbinic notion
(*Tanḥuma, Bereshith* 29, ed. Buber, p. 11a) that, while God
records all of a man's deeds, He lets man himself set his seal to the
record at life's end. The thought is expressed in a comment on
Job 37:7.

21 *If he acquires a good name, etc.* This and the following stanza
are inspired by Ecclesiastes 7:1, 'A good name is better than
precious oil; and the day of death than the day of one's birth.' Cf.
also the Rabbinic comment on that verse:

> You find that man is called by three names: one by which his father
> and mother call him, one by which his fellow-men call him, and
> one which he acquires by himself . . . They asked Solomon: 'What
> is the meaning of Ecclesiastes 7:1?' He answered: 'When a man is
> born, nobody knows what kind of a person he is. But when he dies

after acquiring a good name for himself, having performed an abundance of good deeds, his fellow-Jews will come to busy themselves with his last rites, and proclaim his praises.' (*Tanḥuma, Wayyaqhel*, par. 1.)

CHAPTER X

The All-Inclusive Torah

Between man, as he has been described in our last chapter, and the transcendent God of the Bible there is a gaping gulf. God is God, and man, man. The ways of God are as distant from man's ways, and God's thoughts from man's thoughts, as are the heavens from the earth. (Isaiah 55:8–9.)

But this biblical attitude would never have become biblical *religion* had not the recognition of the existence of this gulf been supplemented by the certainty that it can be bridged, and by the knowledge that, on occasion, the gulf *has* been bridged. The metaphor must not be misunderstood in the sense of obliterating the boundary lines of two distinct entities: God and man. They never merge, neither by an apotheosis of man nor by an 'incarnation' of God. But God, remaining God, makes Himself known to man, who remains man. That is the role of revelation. Basically, revelation, as seen in the Bible, is of two kinds: it is a 'vision' or a 'sight,'[1] and it is the 'Word of the Lord,'[2] or 'Torah,' that is, divine guidance.[3]

Rabbinic Judaism was, therefore, quite faithful to its biblical prototype when, instead of using an ambiguous term like 'revelation,' it spoke, as the occasion demanded, either of *gilluy shekhinah*, the 'revealing of God's Presence,' or of *mattan torah*, the 'giving of divine guidance.'[4]

The Pentateuch, of course, was, for Rabbinic Judaism, the Torah document *par excellence*, possessing a higher authority than the canons of Prophets and Hagiographa. Yet, far from letting this role of the Pentateuch lead them into an almost inevitable espousal of literalist Fundamentalism, the very Rabbis who thus elevated the Pentateuch to a position of supreme arbiter in matters of doctrine and practice also insisted that God's total revelation was *not* confined to the Pentateuch—or even to the Bible as a whole.

They did so by teaching the dogma of the 'Twofold Torah,' which meant that, in addition to the Written Torah, given by God to Moses in the form of the Pentateuch, God also revealed an Oral Torah by means of which alone the Written Torah can be properly understood. The Oral Torah, to be transmitted from master to disciple through the generations, was never meant to be set down in writing. According to Rabbinic teaching, it was only in much later centuries, when the Rabbis had reason to fear that 'the Torah might be forgotten in Israel,' that they found it inescapable to break the law against committing the Oral Torah to writing. What was ultimately written down included the *Mishnah*, the *Gemara*, and the *Midrashim*. And still, even those voluminous collections do not exhaust the totality of the Oral Torah. While there was an argument as to whether the greater part of the Torah was given orally or in writing, Rabbinic Judaism as a whole seems to have adopted the position of Rabbi Yohanan, who said: 'The greater part of the Torah was given orally, and only the minor part in writing.'[5]

Rabbi Yohanan's assertion has had a curious kind of confirmation in recent trends of biblical scholarship. The Scandinavian Bible scholars, in particular, emphasize the role of oral tradition in the evolution of biblical literature. Before anything is written down in an ancient civilization, they argue, it exists in oral form and is transmitted in oral form for generations. Moreover, what does ultimately get written down is never the totality of the tradition, but only a part of it—which, therefore, can be fully understood only to the extent to which we succeed in reconstructing the setting within which it was committed to writing.

It is that totality of the Torah, in both its written and its oral components, which is said by the *Mishnah* to have been received by Moses on Mount Sinai, and to have been passed on by him to Joshua, from whom, in turn, it was received by the elders, the Prophets, and the men of the Great Assembly—who then passed it on to the first heads of the Rabbinic schools.[6]

This, it should be noted, is a dogmatic formulation, not an attempt at historical reconstruction. For one thing, according to the Pentateuchal narrative itself, some laws were revealed before the Sinaitic Revelation, and some laws thereafter. Indeed, the Rabbis hold divergent views on the question whether the Torah was given in individual instalments, or whether it was given as a complete unit—both points of view being held in Rabbinic circles, with neither one declared heretical.[7] For another, the Rabbinic sources quite clearly admit the purely human origin of a number of laws and institutions which are part and parcel of the Oral Torah tradition. They even refer to specific historical circumstances, long after Sinai, when those laws and institutions came into existence.

Thus, for example, the kindling of the Hanukkah lights is not only a part of Rabbinic law, but also one for which the Rabbis ordained a benediction, praising God, 'who has sanctified us by His commandments, and who has commanded us to kindle the Hanukkah lights.' The Rabbis were, of course, fully aware of the fact that Hanukkah does not go back to the Sinaitic Revelation, and that it was the Hasmonean authorities who instituted that festival. Yet they found in the seventeenth chapter of Deuteronomy the warrant needed by the Hasmoneans to ordain the kindling of Hanukkah light—thus linking an innovation of the second century BCE to the revelation received at Sinai.[8]

But that is history—history, moreover, which was not denied even when the dogma was affirmed that the *whole* Torah was given at Sinai. For the 'giving of the Torah' was a concept, a generalization, and therefore not limited to a single concretization or instance.[9]

That 'Sinai' is a cipher for the Rabbis, a kind of shorthand symbol denoting 'divine revelation,' rather than an attempt to give a precise historical reference, should now be clear. The divine origin of the Torah—both written and oral—that was the dogmatic affirmation of Rabbinic Judaism, and that alone. The 'how' and the 'when' of revelation could be debated with impunity as long as the divine origin of the Torah was affirmed. Because of this, the Rabbis also had no dogma about the 'Mosaic authorship' of the Pentateuch, although, as a matter of historical reconstruction but not of dogma, they were convinced that Moses wrote the Pentateuch—with the possible exception of the last few verses of Deuteronomy, describing Moses' death and burial, which, according to some Rabbis, were written by Joshua.[10]

Once, however, 'Sinai,' as a concept, was seen to imply the totality of divine revelation, the biblical narrative about the Sinaitic Revelation—as, for example, in Exodus, chapter 19—could be made to refer to the totality of the Torah, regardless of what the biblical text itself has to say on the subject. What the text itself seems to be reporting is the revelation of the Ten Commandments—and even here, modern scholars are by no means agreed whether the original reference was to the Ten Commandments of Exodus 20:2-14 (or Deuteronomy 5:6-18) or to the so-called Ritual Decalogue, reconstructed by modern scholarship on the basis of Exodus 34:14-26.[11] Thus, when, in Rabbinic Judaism though not yet in the Bible itself, the Feast of Shavu'oth (Pentecost) was celebrated as 'the season of the giving of our Torah,'[12] Exodus 19 and 20 became the synagogal pericope for that occasion; but the Synagogue celebrated more than the Decalogue. It celebrated the *entire* Torah. That is what the author of poem no. 9 meant when he spoke of the 'perfect Law'—the Hebrew word, *kelulah*, meaning not only 'perfect,' but also 'complete' and 'all-inclusive.'

If revelation implies a bridging of the gulf between God and man, then one might expect both sides to be involved in this. The paradigm of revelation would have man ascending and God descending. Thus it is indeed in the narrative of the nineteenth chapter of Exodus. In verse 3, we read that 'Moses went up unto God,' and verse 20 tells us that 'the Lord came down upon mount Sinai.' This, too, is a daring image, made even more daring by all kinds of Rabbinic elaborations which have Moses, in a Promethean role, wrest the Torah from the hands of the angels—or even from the hands of God Himself![13]

Perhaps it was in order to counteract such daring imagery that Rabbi Yosé declared: 'Never did the *Shekhinah* [God's Presence] descend to earth, nor did Moses or Elijah ever ascend to heaven.'[14] But, even if the imagery be accepted, the thought that man is capable of receiving the Word of God is one which seems to contradict ordinary experience as well as the rather somber view of man held by the Rabbis.[15]

> Rabbi Azariah and Rabbi Aḥa said in the name of Rabbi Yoḥanan: 'When Israel heard the word "I" [of the first of the Ten Commandments] at Sinai, their soul flew away—as it is said (Deuteronomy 5:22), "If we hear the voice of the Lord our God any longer, we shall die." And it is said (Song of Songs 5:6): "My soul left me when he spoke."
>
> 'The Word returned to the Holy One, praised be He, and said: "Sovereign of the Universe, You are living and enduring, and Your Torah is living and enduring. But You have sent me to the dead. All of them are dead!"
>
> 'God then sweetened [i.e., made more palatable] the Word for them, as it is said (Psalm 29:4): "The voice of the Lord is in power; the voice of the Lord is in majesty." '
>
> Said Rabbi Hama bar Rabbi Ḥanina: 'For the young, the voice of the Lord was in power; and, for the frail, the voice of the Lord was in majesty.'
>
> Rabbi Simeon ben Yoḥai taught: 'The Torah which the Holy One, praised be He, gave to Israel restored their souls to them, as it is said (Psalm 19:8): "The Torah of the Lord is perfect, restoring the soul." '

The Word of God, therefore, can inflict death as well as bestow life. To be capable of the latter, the Rabbis seem to be saying, the Word of God has to be adapted to the human condition.

That was the Rabbinic view. The Bible itself pictures the human reaction to revelation in more earthly terms. God reveals Himself at Sinai, and Israel—makes the Golden Calf! God's descent, as it were, is easier than man's ascent. Man is only man, and he stumbles in his upward path.

Joseph bar Samuel Tobh 'Elem (Bonfils), the author of poem

no. 9, manages to capture all of the nuances. He has man ascending and God descending. But he also does not conceal the true human condition: 'The comely and beautiful people rebelled at the very moment they heard God speaking!' However, for the poet, as for the Bible and for Judaism as a whole, this does not mean—as it did for some of the early Church Fathers[16]—that the Sinaitic Covenant was never in force, that Israel missed its opportunity of becoming God's chosen people. If the first set of tablets was broken by Moses, God was willing to let Moses bring the people a second set. If the people cannot survive the direct impact of the Word of God, He allows His Word to be mediated and adapted to the human condition.

The constant interaction between God and man is the millennial history of the Torah.

טוביה למרום עלה

מאת ר׳ יוסף בר שמואל טוב עלם

1   טוֹבִיָּה לַמָּרוֹם עָלָה.
וְהוֹרִיד דָּת כְּלוּלָה.
בְּחַג הַשָּׁבֻעוֹת:

2   יָרַד צוּר בְּעַצְמוֹ.
וְנָתַן עֹז לְעַמּוֹ.
בִּרְעָמִים וּזְוָעוֹת:

3   כָּל־עֲצֵי הַיַּעַר.
אֲחָזוּם חִיל וָסַעַר.
וְהָרִים וּגְבָעוֹת:

4   לִמֵּד לְעַם קְדֹשִׁים.
סֵדֶר תְּקוּפוֹת וַחֲדָשִׁים.
וְחֶשְׁבּוֹן הַשָּׁעוֹת:

5 מִכָּל־אֹם חֲבָבָם.
וּלְהַר סִינַי קֵרְבָם.
אֵל לְמוֹשָׁעוֹת:

6 נְשָׂאָם בְּכַנְפֵי נְשָׁרִים.
שׁוֹכֵן בְּרוּם אוּרִים.
וּמִתַּחַת זְרֹעֹת:

7 סוֹרְרִים בְּעֵת שָׁמְעָם.
צְבִי תִּפְאֶרֶת עָם.
יִרְגְּזוּן יְרִיעוֹת:

8 עֲלוּבִים חָפוּ רֹאשָׁם.
וְלַהֲרֹגָה צוּר הִקְדִּישָׁם.
בִּפְרוֹעַ פְּרָעוֹת:

9 פְּרִישַׂת הוֹד שַׁלְמָה.
וּרְקוּעַת גֹּבַהּ אֲדָמָה.
שְׁתִּיהֶן נוֹגְעוֹת:

10 צַדִּיק הַר כָּפָה.
עֲלֵי נָאוָה וְיָפָה.
כְּגִגִּית וְכִירִיעוֹת:

11 קָשְׁבוּ עַם בְּחִירִים.
חֻקִּים וּמִשְׁפָּטִים יְשָׁרִים.
לְאֹזֶן הַשְּׁמָעֹת:

12 רָם בְּחַסְדּוֹ שְׁמָרָם.
מִכַּף כָּל־צוֹרְרָם.
וּמִגְּזֵרוֹת רָעוֹת:

13 שָׁלַח אוֹתוֹת וּמוֹפְתִים.
וְהִנְחִילָם דָּתוֹת חֲרוּתִים.
בְּחָכְמָה וּבְדֵעוֹת:

14 תִּפְאַרְתָּם הִגְדִּיל לְמַעְלָה.
לְתִתָּם לְשֵׁם וְלִתְהִלָּה.
כְּבִרְכַּת כּוֹס יְשׁוּעוֹת:

9 'MOSES WENT UP ON HIGH'
by Joseph bar Samuel Tobh 'Elem (Bonfils)

1 Moses went up on high,
   and brought down the perfect Law
      on the Feast of Shavu'oth.

2 The Rock Himself descended,
   and gave strength unto His people
      with thunders and with earthquakes.

3 All the trees of the forest
   were seized by fear and trembling,
      and also the hills and the mountains.

4 He taught the holy people
   the order of solstices and months
      and the reckoning of the hours.

5 He loved them more than all other nations,
   and brought them to Mount Sinai,
      the God of salvation.

6 He carried them on eagles' wings,
   He that dwells in lofty heights;
      and underneath are the everlasting arms.

7 They, the comely and beautiful people,
    rebelled at the very moment they heard God speaking;
        the very heavens shook.

8 The shamed ones covered their heads,
    and the Rock devoted them to the slaughter,
        when the time for punishment came.

9 The majestic expanse of the sky
    and a lofty stretch of earth,
        they were touching each other.

10 The Righteous One turned the mountain
    over the fair and comely people
        like a barrel and like curtains.

11 The chosen people hearkened
    to upright statutes and ordinances
        with an attentive ear.

12 The Lofty One, in His mercy,
    protected them from the hand of all their enemies
        and also from evil decrees.

13 He sent signs and wonders,
    and bequeathed to them engraved laws
        in wisdom and in knowledge.

14 He greatly magnified their glory,
    making them famous and praised,
        like the blessing of the cup of salvation.

Commentary

The text of this poem may be found in Arthur Davis and
Herbert M. Adler, eds, *Service of the Synagogue*, Pentecost

THE ALL-INCLUSIVE TORAH

volume, 12th ed., London, 1949, pp. 144–5. Its listing in
Davidson's *Thesaurus* is in vol. 2, p. 189, no. 257.

Joseph bar Samuel Tobh 'Elem (Bonfils), born in Narbonne in
the eleventh century, served as a Rabbi in Limoges. He is noted
both for his contributions to Jewish legal literature and for his
synagogal poetry—the latter drawing heavily upon the Scripture
exegesis of the *Midrash*. See Leopold Zunz, *Literaturgeschichte der
synagogalen Poesie*, Berlin, 1865, pp. 129–38.

The selection offered here is one section of Joseph bar Samuel's
Ma'arabhoth (poetic embellishments of the two benedictions
before, and the two benedictions, after the evening *Shema'*) for
Shavu'oth Eve. The poet has chosen a very intricate poetic
scheme—we are talking about the composition as a whole, and
not just about the selection presented here—in which he links his
treatment of the Sinaitic Revelation with the main contents of
the standard benedictions of the evening service. The opening
words of each verse in Exodus 19:19–20:15, including the
opening words of each of the Ten Commandments, form the
opening words of the poet's sentences. This scheme is integrated
with another poetic scheme in which a complete acrostic of the
Hebrew alphabet is produced, as well as an acrostic of the poet's
name.

The scheme, however, is interrupted in the first poetic insert in
the first benediction after the *Shema'*. Here, and this is the section
we are reproducing, the poet merely completes the alphabetical
acrostic from *teth* to *taw*, and adopts a meter and rhyme quite
different from those of the rest of this composition. It is a meditation on the roles of both God and man in the Sinaitic Revelation.
There are three Hebrew words in each of the first two stichoi of
every stanza, and two—three in the last stanza—in the last
stichos which invariably ends in '-oth'.

1 *Moses.* The Hebrew text has 'Tobiah'—on the basis of b. *Sotah*
12a, where, in a playful interpretation of Exodus 2:2 (*watére otho
ki tobh hu*), Moses is said to have also been called Tobiah. It should
be borne in mind that the poet's scheme required this stanza to
begin with the letter *teth*.

120

the perfect Law. The Hebrew, *kelulah*, also has the sense of 'complete' and 'all-inclusive.'

2, also stanza **3** The 'earth-shaking' aspects of the Sinaitic Revelation, indicated in such passages as Exodus 19:16–18, played a significant role in the Rabbinic typology of Revelation. See Jakob J. Petuchowski, '*Qol Adonai*: a study in Rabbinic theology,' *Zeitschrift für Religions- und Geistesgeschichte*, 24 (1972), pp. 13–21.

strength, as in Psalm 29:11, is identified by the Rabbis with Torah. See *Siphré to Deuteronomy*, ed. Finkelstein, p. 398, note.

4 *the order of solstices and months*. According to the Rabbinic interpretation of Exodus 12:2, God revealed to Moses and Aaron, by way of setting the stage for the first Passover, the entire system of the Jewish calendar (as it was later calculated in the Rabbinic period). See *Mekhilta, Masekheth dePisha* 1 and 2, ed. Horovitz-Rabin, pp. 6–9. This 'commandment of the calendar' was the very first commandment which Israel received as a people. See Rashi's comment on Genesis 1:1. Since, moreover, the Rabbis considered the whole Torah to have been revealed at Sinai, and not just the Ten Commandments, the poet, here addressing himself to the *content* of the Sinaitic Revelation, dwells on this 'first commandment' given to Israel.

6 *He carried them on eagles' wings*. Cf. Exodus 19:4.

and underneath are the everlasting arms. Cf. Deuteronomy 33:27. The transcendent God ('He that dwells in lofty heights') is, in the Jewish view, concerned with man, supporting him in his lowly situation. The Hebrew original does·not have the word 'everlasting,' but, since the reference is obviously to Deuteronomy 33:27, we felt justified in supplying what the poet intended but did not say.

7, also stanza **8** The reference is to the Golden Calf narrative, in Exodus, chapter 32, which describes both the people's idolatry at the very moment when Moses was receiving the Torah, and the terrible punishment meted out to the people upon Moses' return. The poet's use of the word 'rebelled' (*sorerim*) echoes the identical word in Psalm 68:19, the Shavu'oth Psalm *par excellence*, which, in *Exodus Rabbah* 33:2, is understood by the Rabbis to refer to the people's idolatrous conduct at the time of the Sinaitic Revelation.

Similarly, his use of 'the shamed ones' (*'alubhim*) recalls Ulla's exclamation in b. *Gittin* 36b, 'Shameful (*'alubhah*) is the bride who commits fornication while still under her bridal canopy!'—a description referred by the Talmud to Israel's idolatrous conduct while they were still encamped at the foot of Mount Sinai. Israel's rebellious behavior is an essential element of the poet's treatment of the very 'paradox' of revelation: man ascends and God descends, heaven and earth are meeting—and man, in his contrariness, shows himself incapable of absorbing the immediate impact of God's word.

the very heavens shook. Literally: 'the curtains do tremble' (Habakkuk 3:7). The Habakkuk verse is part of the Prophetic Lesson (*haphtarah*) on the second day of Pentecost. But Psalm 104:2 speaks of God's 'stretching out the heavens like a curtain,' a simile on which our translation is based.

8 *when the time for punishment came.* Hebrew: *biphro'a pera'oth*. The phrase comes from Judges 5:2, where its meaning is unclear. Suggested translations include: 'when men let their hair grow wild,' 'when the leaders took the lead,' and 'the avenging.' Whatever the meaning of this phrase may be in Judges 5:2, it is clear that our poet has in mind the *Niph'al* use of *para'*, which, in Rabbinic Hebrew, means 'to collect payment,' 'to exact punishment.'

10 *The Righteous One turned the mountain ... like a barrel.* Rabbinic literature describes two different states of mind in which Israel accepted the Torah at Sinai. According to one account (*Siphré to Deuteronomy, pisqa* 343, ed. Finkelstein, pp. 395ff.), Israel accepted the Torah gladly and voluntarily after other nations had rejected it. According to another account, in b. *Shabbath* 88a, which is presupposed here, God held Mount Sinai 'like a barrel' over Israel, saying to them: 'If you accept the Torah, well and good. If not, this will be your burial place.'

fair and comely. These are two of the attributes of the beloved in the Song of Songs. According to the Rabbinic interpretation of that biblical book, the beloved is Israel.

13 *engraved laws.* According to Exodus 32:16, the laws were 'engraved upon the tablets.' The word 'engraved' (*haruth*) led to the Rabbinic pun in b. *'Erubhin* 54a: 'Do not read *ḥaruth* ("engraved"), but *ḥeruth* ("freedom").' That is to say, in the observance of the Sinaitic Law you will achieve true freedom. Any Rabbinic Jew, and that would include our poet, who quotes Exodus 32:16, is familiar with that pun and its profound message.

14 *like the blessing of the cup of salvation*. Cf. Psalm 116:13. The reference to the cup of salvation makes little sense in this stanza. There are a number of possible reasons why the poet might have used that phrase here. (a) It gives him another phrase ending in '*-oth*' to carry out his rhyme scheme. (b) The word 'salvation' (*yeshu'oth*) is taken up again immediately in the next paragraph of the over-all *ma'arabhoth* scheme, in which the poet begins to spell out his name, using the word *yeshu'oth* for the letter *yod*. (c) The poem is an insert in the first benediction after the *Shema'*, the major theme of which is the Exodus from Egypt, an instance and prototype of divine 'salvation.' By the rulings of Rabbinic law— i.e., the '*halakhic* compromise' which we discussed in chapter I— the poet was obliged to link up his treatment of an 'extraneous' subject with the main burden of the benediction he had interrupted.

CHAPTER XI

Waiting for 'the End'

One of the questions which, according to Raba, a man will be asked 'when he is led in for judgment,' i.e., after he has completed his earthly course, is: 'Have you looked forward to salvation?'[1] Man, that is to say, is expected to be an optimist, to find compensation for his sufferings in the certainty of an ultimate salvation. Life is not without purpose, history not bereft of design.

Admittedly, the world experienced by man is not as 'very good' as, according to Genesis 1:31, it was intended to be. But the imperfections are only temporary. Potentially, the world is still 'very good,' and, one day, it will be so in actuality. After all, God, the Creator and Revealer, is also God, the Redeemer.

Thus was the messianic hope born. Actually, the Bible gives us two different, and apparently contradictory, versions of that hope. On the one hand, there was the expectation that, in the normal course of events, things would get better. This development was expected to take place on the plane of history. Sometimes it was characterized by the figure of the ideal king, the Messiah. At other times, the ideal age of the future, the 'latter days,' when nations beat their swords into ploughshares and their spears into pruning-hooks, was pictured without any reference to the particular form of government under which men will live then.[2]

But the Bible also knows of another expectation. According to the Book of Daniel, prototypical of apocalyptic literature, the 'kingdom of the saints of the Most High' will burst miraculously

—vertically, as it were—into the normal course of history, and bring history, as we know it, to a predetermined End. Since that End is predetermined by God, there would seem to be little that man can do, one way or another, to bring it about. At best, man might attempt, on the basis of mysterious and mystifying hints, such as the Book of Daniel and similar writings provide, to figure out and calculate just when that apocalyptic End is going to burst in upon us.

The Rabbis inherited both biblical notions. Some of them may have championed the one biblical notion, while others championed the other. Changing political circumstances may well have had something to do with bringing one point of view to the fore at one time, and another point of view at another time. No doubt, the messianic expectations took one form before the Bar Kokhba rebellion (132–135 CE), when some Jews thought that they could break the Roman yoke, and when Rabbi Akiba hailed Bar Kokhba as the Messiah, and quite a different form after that rebellion had come to grief.

But, over and above this linking of the messianic hope to the changing political fortunes of the nation, there is discernible a more general attempt on the part of the Rabbis to reconcile and to harmonize the two inherited and contradictory biblical visions of messianic fulfilment. That is to say, the Rabbis both accepted the concept of a predetermined End, and, at the same time, they refused to deny man's share in helping to bring it about.

On the verse in Isaiah 60:22, 'I, the Lord, will hasten it in its time,' Rabbi Joshua ben Levi, in the third century CE, made the following comment: 'If Israel merits it, "I will hasten it." And if Israel does not merit it, it will be "in its—predetermined—time." '[3] The assumption here is that the predetermined End is far off in the distant future, but that, by means of meritorious acts, Israel might persuade God, as it were, to revise His schedule, and to bring about the End much earlier than originally planned.

A similar thought was expressed by Rabh, also in the third century. Rabh, however, reversed the sequence. According to him, 'all dates calculated for the End have already gone by.' The End just did not materialize—no doubt, because man was in no fit state to experience it. But the messianic promise still stands, and, with all the calculated times for the End already gone by, messianic fulfilment now depends solely on man's 'repentance and good deeds.'[4]

In this manner, some of the leading Rabbis tried to do justice to both Isaiah and Daniel. The attempt has remained para-digmatic for Rabbinic Judaism as a whole. The messianic ful-filment will be the result of a joint endeavor of both God and man. God will send the Messiah, but man must be spiritually fit to receive him. Unless, of course, there should be a generation which is so totally wicked and heading for self-destruction that God simply will have to send the Messiah to save humankind from destroying itself—just as the Messiah would inevitably come if the world were ever to be inhabited by a totally righteous generation. That, at any rate, was the opinion of yet another third-century teacher, Rabbi Yoḥanan, who said: 'The son of David will come only in a generation that is either altogether righteous or altogether wicked.'[5]

Since, as yet, no generation has considered itself either com-pletely righteous or completely wicked, the Jew continues to live in a pre-messianic tension. He knows, on the one hand, that he is living in an unredeemed world, and, on the other hand, he is fortified by divine promises of salvation. The promised End is a certainty, but so is the existential experience of Exile. This tension is constantly reinforced not only by the actual historical cir-cumstances in which a Jew might find himself at any given time, but also by the liturgical year in which the Jew lives.

Fast days in commemoration of past national disasters and destructions of Jerusalem, with their appropriate Scriptural lectionaries and liturgical expressions, alternate with celebrations of past deliverances and their strengthening of future hopes. The day of disaster *par excellence* is the ninth day of the month of Abh. It commemorates the destruction of both the first and the second Temples as well as other bleak moments in Jewish history—among them the expulsion of the Jews from Spain in 1492. But the Ninth of Abh does not simply 'happen' in the Jewish calendar. The Jew is psychologically prepared for its coming. For three

Sabbaths before the Ninth of Abh, the Jew has been listening to especially selected Prophetic Lessons of rebuke from Jeremiah and Isaiah, the 'Three *Haphtaroth* of Punishment.'[6] Yet, once the Black Fast is over, the synagogue, for the next seven Sabbaths, will resound with Deutero-Isaiah's words of comfort and hope, when the 'Seven *Haphtaroth* of Consolation' are being read.[7] The message of consolation is as real as is the re-living of the disaster and the premonition of disaster which preceded it.

The message of consolation is real, but the condition of Exile abides. And the result? There are several possible results. Despair is one of them—but hardly an option for the Jew who believes that, before the judgment seat of God, he will be asked: 'Have you looked forward to salvation?' Another possibility is impatience with the Rabbinic answer that messianic fulfilment is the achievement of both God and man—an impatience which, in the nineteenth century, led to Reform Judaism, Zionism, and socialism, all of them secular versions of the messianic hope, in which man himself assumed the role which traditionally God was expected to play. A third option, and that is the one chosen by Eleazar Kallir, the author of poem no. 10, a poem composed for the second Sabbath of the period when the 'Seven *Haphtaroth* of Consolation' are read, is to let the promise of salvation become so vivid, to hear God Himself speak through the Prophetic lection, that the present troubles are made to look as though they were practically already transcended.

But, of course, until now they have never been transcended in fact. Messiah did not come. Exile abides. Yet so does the hope for redemption and the obligation to look forward to salvation. Waiting for the End has thus become the typically Jewish posture—and particularly so for a Jewry which, on the one hand, was persecuted by Christian nations, and which, on the other, was constantly assured by those same Christians that the Messiah had already come. It was in 'waiting for the End' that the Jew voiced his opposition to the dominant faith, his challenging declaration that the world was as yet unredeemed.

That waiting has not always been of a patient kind. Time and again, pseudo-messiahs arose within the ranks of Jewry 'to push the End,' as the Rabbinic phrase has it. Such pseudo-messiahs were never without their supporters; and the inevitable disappointment was always severe. And yet, even the pseudo-messiahs helped to keep the messianic hope alive.

Still, much more effective than the pseudo-messiahs were the divine promises in Scripture. However, those promises were not without their intrinsic problems. After all, the Church relied on the same prophecies, and claimed that they had already been fulfilled. Moreover, generations longing for immediate redemption could obtain no definite answers from the Prophets as to when redemption would, at long last, come. That is the setting in which Abraham Ibn Ezra, in the twelfth century, composed poem no. 11. Contrary to Christian claims that the Messiah had already come, Ibn Ezra knows that the messianic prophecies will be fulfilled only once the Ingathering of the Exiles has taken place; and, in opposition to some of his 'enlightened' contemporaries who may have become unconcerned about the messianic hope, he finds comfort in God's explicit promise. And, with relief, he continues to wait for the End.

אם הבנים

מאת ר' אלעזר הקליר

א

1 אֵם הַבָּנִים כְּיוֹנָה מְנַהֶמֶת

2 בַּלֵּב מִתְאוֹנֶנֶת וּבַפֶּה מִתְרָעֶמֶת:

3 גּוֹעָה בִּבְכִי וּבְמַר נוֹאֶמֶת

4 דְּמָעוֹת מַזֶּלֶת וְדוֹמֶמֶת וְנִדְהֶמֶת:

5 הִשְׁלִיכַנִי בַעֲלִי וְסָר מֵעָלַי

6 וְלֹא זָכַר אַהֲבַת כְּלוּלַי:

7 זֵרַנִי וּפִזְּרַנִי מֵעַל גְּבוּלַי

8 חָדָה עָלַי כָּל־תּוֹלְלַי:

128

טְרָפַנִי כְּנִדָּה וּמִפָּנָיו הִדְּחַנִי 9
יְקָשַׁנִי בְּכֹבֶד וְלֹא הֱנִיחַנִי: 10
כָּלוּ עֵינַי בְּתוֹכָחוֹת וּכְחַנִי 11
לָמָּה לָנֶצַח עֲזָבַנִי שְׁכֵחַנִי: 12

ב

מַה תִּתְאוֹנְנִי עָלַי יוֹנָתִי 13
נֶטַע חֶמֶד עֲרוּגַת גַּנָּתִי: 14
שִׂיחַ פְּלוּלַיִךְ כְּבָר עָנִיתִי 15
עָטוּר בָּךְ כְּאָז חָנִיתִי: 16

פָּנִיתִי אֵלַיִךְ בְּרַחֲמַי הָרַבִּים 17
צְעוֹד בְּשַׁעַר בַּת רַבִּים: 18
קָמַיִךְ אֲשֶׁר עָלַיִךְ מִתְרַבִּים 19
רָעַשְׁתִּי הֱיוֹת כְּעָשָׁן כָּבִים: 20

שְׁחוֹרָתִי לָעַד לֹא אֶזְנָחֵךְ 21
שֵׁנִית אוֹסִיף יָד וְאֶקָחֵךְ: 22
תַּמּוּ וְסָפוּ דְבָרֵי וְכוּחֵךְ 23
תַּמָּתִי לֹא אֶעֱזְבֵךְ וְלֹא אֶשְׁכָּחֵךְ: 24

'LO, MOTHER ZION'
by Eleazar Kallir

I

Lo, Mother Zion, like a dove she is cooing.
In her heart there's a grumble, in her mouth a complaint.
Bursting out crying and bitterly speaking,
She is stunned as in silence she is shedding her tears.

'My husband has dropped me, and has now departed.
The love of my nuptials he thinks of no more.

7 He has cast and dispersed me away from my country,
8 Rejoicing my foes anent my distress.

9 He cast me from him like some unclean woman;
10 He trapped me with burdens, and gave me no rest.
11 My eyes have failed from reproofs he inflicted.
12 Why did he forsake me, forget me for aye?

II

13 My dove, why do you grumble about me,
14 You plant of desire and bed of my garden?
15 Your prayerful plea already I've answered.
16 In your very midst I'm encamped as of old.

17 To you I am turning in greatness of mercy,
18 As toward Jerusalem I steadfastly pace.
19 For the increasing numbers of those who attacked you
20 I caused an uproar: they vanish like smoke.

21 My comely and black one! I never will leave you.
22 Once again with my hand will I take you to wife.
23 Completed and ended be your words of contention.
24 My pure one! 'Tis you I'll not leave nor forget.

Commentary

This poem is part of a *qerobhah* (i.e., poetic embellishment of the *'Amidah*) for the second Sabbath after the Ninth of Abh, when Isaiah 49:14ff. is read as the Prophetic Lesson. The author has been identified as Eleazar Kallir (sixth century?). The poem is not now a part of the liturgy of any of the existing rites, but has been preserved in manuscript form, Oxford MS. 2736/M. It was edited and published by M. Zulay in *Mibhḥar Hashibh'im*, Tel-Aviv, 1947, pp. 26-7, and has been reprinted in Aaron Mirsky, ed., *Yalqut Hapiyyutim*, Jerusalem and Tel-Aviv, 1958, pp. 24-5.

The poem contains an alphabetical acrostic, each line beginning
with the succeeding letter of the Hebrew alphabet, with two lines
for each of the last two letters.

Of the six stanzas of this poem, the first three are Israel's complaint to God, and the last three are God's reply to Israel.

1 *Lo, Mother Zion.* The Hebrew original has 'the mother of
children' (Psalm 113:9), which, like the antecedent 'barren
woman' of the same Psalms verse, is understood by some of the
Rabbis as a reference to Zion. See *Yalqut Shime'oni*, Psalms,
no. 873.

13 *My dove.* Cf. Song of Songs 2:14, understood by the Rabbis
as a reference to Israel.

14 *plant of desire.* Cf. Isaiah 5:7.

bed of my garden. Cf. Song of Songs 6:2, also understood as a
reference to Israel.

18 *Jerusalem.* The Hebrew original has 'by the gate of Bath-
rabbim' (Song of Songs 7:5). Cf. Rashi ad loc. for the Rabbinic
interpretation of this name as Jerusalem.

21 *My comely and black one.* The Hebrew original has 'my black
one' only. But the reference is obviously to Song of Songs 1:5.

24 *My pure one.* Cf. Song of Songs 5:2.

אם אויבי יאמרו רע לי

מאת ר' אברהם אבן עזרא

1	אִם אוֹיְבַי יֹאמְרוּ רַע לִי
2	וְאָמַרְתִּי מָטָה רַגְלִי
3	אֱלֹהֵי אַבְרָהָם אֵלִי
4	וּפַחַד יִצְחָק הָיָה לִי:
5	בִּינוֹתִי בְּסִפְרֵי נְבִיאִים
6	וְדִבְרֵי יְשַׁעְיָה בְּמִכְתָּבוֹ
7	הָיוּ לְפָנַי נִקְרָאִים
8	כִּי קְרוֹבָה יְשׁוּעָה לָבוֹא

9   הֵן דֹּרוֹת עֹבְרִים וּבָאִים

10   וְעַם אֵל עֹמֵד בְּמַכְאֹבוֹ

11   כִּי אֶלֶף שָׁנִים פְּלָאִים

12   יָרַד וּבִמְרִירוּת לְבָבוֹ

13   יֹאמַר אִם־תִּגְאֵל גְּאַל וְאִם־

14   לֹא תִגְאַל הַגִּידָה לִּי:

15   רָאִיתָ יְחֶזְקֵאל מַרְאוֹת

16   וְעָלַי נָשָׂאתָ מְשָׁלִים

17   הֲבִקַּשְׁתָּ דְּבָרַי לִרְאוֹת

18   וְשָׁאַלְתָּ לִבְנֵי אֵלִים

19   עַד־מָתַי קֵץ הַפְּלָאוֹת

20   כִּי לֹא בָאָה שְׁנַת גְּאוּלִים

21   הֲשִׁיבַנִי עַל־פִּי נְבוּאוֹת

22   מַה־יֵּשׁ בְּיַד הַמַּשְׂכִּילִים

23   לַעֲשׂוֹת וַאדֹנָי הֶעֱלִים

24   מִמֶּנִּי וְלֹא הִגִּיד לִי:

25   מִי־יִתֶּן־לִי וְאֶתְחַבָּר

26   עִם דָּנִיֵּאל אִישׁ־חֲמֻדוֹת

27   אֲשֶׁר יָדַע פֵּשֶׁר דָּבָר

28   וְהֵבִין בְּכָל־מָשָׁל וְחִידוֹת

29   אֶתְחַנֶּן־לוֹ בְּלֵב־נִשְׁבָּר

30   וְאֶשְׁאָלֶנּוּ עַל־אֹדוֹת

31   הַקֵּץ לִרְאוֹת אִם־עָבָר

32   וְאִם עוֹד נְבוּאוֹתָיו עֲתִידוֹת

33   אַנְשֵׁי לֵבָב יֹאמְרוּ לִי

34   מַה־זֶּה תִּשְׁאַל וְהוּא פֶּלִיא:

35   נִבְעֲרוּ חֲכָמַי וּנְבוֹנָי

36   וְאִישׁ מֵהֶם לֹא יָדַע מָה

37 וּמֵרֹב בְּכִי חָשְׁכוּ עֵינָי
38 כִּי עֵת פְּדוּתִי נֶעְלָמָה
39 וָאֲחַפֵּשׂ בְּתוֹרַת אֲדֹנָי
40 וָאֶמְצָא חֶפְצִי שָׁמָּה
41 כִּי אֵל יָשִׁיב שְׁבוּת הֲמוֹנִי
42 וְלוּ נִדְּחוּ בְּקַצְוֵי אֲדָמָה
43 זֹאת הָיְתָה־לִּי נֶחָמָה
44 עַל־כֵּן אֲדַבְּרָה וְיִרְוַח־לִי:

II 'IF MY ENEMIES SPEAK EVIL'
by Abraham Ibn Ezra

1 If my enemies speak evil of me,
2 And I say, 'My foot is slipping,'
3 The God of Abraham is still my God,
4 And the Fear of Isaac is on my side.

5 I have studied the books of the Prophets,
6 And the words of Isaiah in his writing
7 Were read in my presence, saying:
8 'For My salvation is near to come.'
9 Yet generations pass away and are born
10 While God's people remains in its pain.
11 For a millennium, quite appallingly,
12 It has sunk; and, in the bitterness of its heart,
13 It says: 'If You will redeem, then redeem! But
14 If You will not redeem, then tell me.'

15 O Ezekiel, you have seen visions,
16 And you have told parables about me.
17 Have you also sought to look after my cause?
18 Have you asked the angels about it?
19 How long will it be until the wonderful End?
20 For the year of redemption has failed to come.
21 Through prophecies he answered me:

22 'What is there for wise men
23 To do, seeing that the Lord has hid it
24 From me, and has not told me?'

25 O would that I could keep company
26 With Daniel, the man greatly beloved,
27 Who of everything knew the meaning,
28 And understood all proverbs and riddles.
29 With a broken heart I would entreat him,
30 And ask him concerning
31 The End; to see if it has passed us by,
32 Or whether his predictions are yet to be.
33 But intelligent men are telling me:
34 'Why do you ask, seeing the matter is hidden?'

35 My sages and thinkers, they are so dull;
36 Not one among them knows a thing.
37 And through much weeping my eyes became dim,
38 For the time of my redemption is concealed.
39 So I searched for myself in the Torah of the Lord,
40 And there I found what I desired:
41 That God will restore my captive multitudes,
42 Though they be dispersed to the ends of the earth.
43 This indeed became my comfort.
44 Therefore will I speak, and I shall have relief.

Commentary

This poem may be found in H. Brody and K. Albrecht, eds,
The New-Hebrew School of Poets of the Spanish-Arabian Epoch,
London, 1906, pp. 155–6, and in H. Brody, ed., *Kuntras ha-
Pijutim nach der Machsor-Vitry-Handschrift*, Nürnberg, 1923, p. 36.
Its listing in Davidson's *Thesaurus* is in vol. 1, p. 239, no. 5159.
From Davidson's references it would appear that, at the present
time, the Yemenite liturgy is the only one which utilizes this
poem as part of the worship service.

The author, Abraham Ibn Ezra (1089–1164), was a much travelled and erudite personality. See the article about him in the *Encyclopaedia Judaica*, vol. 8, cols 1163–70; and cf. Leopold Zunz, *Literaturgeschichte der synagogalen Poesie*, Berlin, 1865, pp. 207–14. Abraham Ibn Ezra's fame rests more on his commentaries to the Bible than on his poetry; yet, as Zunz (loc. cit.) has shown, a considerable portion of the latter has survived.

The poem has both rhyme and meter. The opening letters of the first four stanzas contain the acrostic 'Abram' (= Abraham). A skilful use of biblical phrases, often taken out of context, marks this poem.

Zunz (op. cit., p. 213) surmises, on the basis of lines 11 and 12 where 'a millennium' of Jewish deterioration is mentioned, that the poem was written 'shortly after 1120'. But why Ibn Ezra should be dating the decline from the year 120, rather than from 70, Zunz does not say.

The poet's conception of appealing from the Prophets to God Himself, as though the Prophets were not also the messengers of God's Word, is a rather daring one. It does, however, have its prototype—albeit not in connection with the messianic redemption, but in connection with repentance—in pal. *Makkoth* 2, 6 (p. 31d), where God, quoting the Book of Psalms, gives the desired answer which Proverbs and Ezekiel have failed to provide. In a parallel version, *Yalqut Shime'oni*, Psalm 25, no. 702, God's answer also overrides a quotation from the Pentateuch—which, perhaps, is even more daring than Ibn Ezra's finding God's answer in Deuteronomy.

1 *If my enemies speak evil of me.* A quotation from Psalm 41:6.
2 *My foot is slipping.* A quotation from Psalm 94:18.
3-4 Cf. Genesis 31:42, 'Except the God of my father, the God of Abraham, and the Fear of Isaac, had been on my side.' 'Fear of Isaac' is a designation of the Deity.
8 *For My salvation is near to come.* A quotation from Isaiah 56:1. The poet, for reasons of meter, omits the possessive suffix 'my' from the biblical quotation, but the reader is obviously meant to think of that quotation in its original form.

11–12 *quite appallingly, It has sunk.* Cf. Lamentations 1:9, 'She [i.e., Jerusalem] has sunk appallingly.'

13–14 Cf. Ruth 4:4, 'If you are willing to redeem it, redeem! But if you [Masoretic text reads "he"] will not redeem, tell me.'

19 *How long will it be until the wonderful End?* The Hebrew, a quotation from Daniel 12:6, literally says: 'How long shall it be to the end of the wonders?' But the Hebrew *ketz hapela-oth* also lends itself to the translation given here. See Eliezer Ben-Yehudah, *Thesaurus*, vol. 12, p. 6078. 'The End' is, of course, the eschaton.

23–4 Cf. II Kings 4:27, 'The Lord has hid it from me, and has not told me.'

26 *Daniel, the man greatly beloved.* A quotation from Daniel 10:11.

31 *to see if it has passed us by.* Cf. b. *Sanhedrin* 97b, where Rabh, using a somewhat different terminology, says: 'All the calculated dates for the End have passed, and the matter now depends only on repentance and good deeds.'

34 *Why do you ask, seeing the matter is hidden?* Cf. Judges 13:18, 'Why do you ask after my name, seeing it is hidden?'

41–2 Cf. Deuteronomy 30:3, 4, 'Then the Lord your God . . . will restore your captivity . . . Even if your outcasts are at the ends of the world [lit. "heaven"], from there the Lord your God will gather you.'

Epilogue

Two thousand and sixty pages in Israel Davidson's monumental *Thesaurus of Mediaeval Hebrew Poetry*[1] are almost exclusively devoted to a mere bibliographical listing of the *piyyutim*; and that listing is not even complete. Further poetic creations have come to light, particularly through published *genizah* fragments, since Davidson first published his *magnum opus* in the first third of this century. Of this vast body of literature, the eleven poems which we have reproduced in this volume do not presume to offer even a foretaste. But it is important for the reader to know how all-pervasive a phenomenon the *piyyut*, at one time, constituted in Jewish religious life.

Of course, no single community ever included all of the available *piyyutim* in its services. Indeed, it is clearly one of the dividing lines between one liturgical rite and another that some *piyyutim* are recited and that others are excluded. Some curious results emerge from a comparative study of the various rites. It is, for example, generally conceded that, from a purely aesthetic point of view, the poetic creations of the Spanish and Portuguese Synagogue are far superior to those of Ashkenazi Jewry. Yet comparatively few *piyyutim* have actually been incorporated into the Sepharadi service, whereas *piyyutim* tend to proliferate in the Ashkenazi rite. Thus, in a standard edition of the latter,[2] one hundred pages are devoted to the Morning and Additional Services of the first day of Passover. Of those one hundred pages, fully twenty-four, or almost a quarter of the entire service, are taken up by *piyyutim*! The comparable ritual of the Sepharadi tradition has no more than three pages of *piyyutim*.[3]

Nascent Reform Judaism in the nineteenth century won its spurs by waging a battle against the *piyyutim*. In its effort to reduce the duration of the services to a span of time which would match the span of attention and devotion of the worshipper, Reform Judaism saw in the *piyyutim* that element of the traditional liturgy which could most easily be shed. Particularly so, because, as we have seen in chapter I, there was ample precedent for opposition to the *piyyutim* in the legal literature of traditional Judaism.

Nor did Reform Judaism remain alone in that endeavor. Orthodox authorities in the Western world followed suit. Thus, in 1856, Salomon Ullman, the Grand Rabbin of France, in conjunction with the Grand Rabbins of the various French consistories, eliminated the *piyyutim* from all services with the exception of the High Holy Days.[4] And in England, Chief Rabbi Nathan Adler (1803–90) sanctioned the omission of many a *piyyut*.[5]

Still, the *piyyutim* did have their function. For example, the standard liturgy is identical for all the Three Pilgrim Festivals. With the exception of the naming of the given festival in two or three prayers, and with the exception of the different Scripture pericopes, there is no difference between a Passover service and a service for Pentecost or Tabernacles. In the traditional synagogue, it was one of the functions of the *piyyutim*, together with the synagogal tunes reserved for given occasions, to bring home to the worshipper the distinctiveness of each specific festival.

Hymns, meditations and modern poems in the vernacular have, since the nineteenth century, taken the place of most of the *piyyutim* in the liturgy of Liberal and Reform Judaism. But even here, a few of the old *piyyutim* have been retained or re-introduced —if they met the new standards of aesthetics, brevity and intelligibility. It was the application of those standards which, ever since the 1819 publication of the Hamburg Temple prayerbook, made the Reformers, even in the Ashkenazi realm, partial to the poetic creations of Spanish Jewry.

Yet by and large, and not excluding many an Orthodox Jewish community, interest in the *piyyutim* has shifted from the synagogue to the classroom and the scholar's study. On the whole, *piyyutim* tend to be more significant as historical documents of an earlier piety than as vehicles of contemporary religious expression. Thus removed from the arena of battle, *piyyutim* have begun to be appreciated for the light they can shed on the development of the Hebrew language, on various forms of the triennial cycle of Pentateuchal readings, on historical events, on the relationship of various Jewries to their environments, on the evolution of Jewish liturgy, and—as we hope that the present volume has demonstrated—on the diversity of theological views sanctioned by Judaism's pluralistic tradition.

While, on occasion, a modern Jewish worshipper may voice the desire for a liturgy which would give expression to a uniform theological position, usually of a non-Orthodox kind, it is ironical that the Orthodox liturgical tradition stands forth as the classical representative of theological pluralism. It could not have been different. A liturgical compendium which is the product of centuries and millennia, rather than the work of a single man or of a specially appointed committee, must of necessity reflect the manifold changes in religious mood and theological consensus which the vagaries of a long and eventful history have wrought among the Jewish faith-community. Thus it could happen that poems expressing unconventional theological positions became embedded within a framework of standard liturgical formulae speaking in quite different accents. Some of the chapters in this book have tried to illustrate this.

But this peculiarity of Jewish worship has been in evidence from the very beginning, going back to biblical prayer itself. There is a certain dialectic in classical Jewish prayer, an awareness of tension, of pulls in opposite directions. There is an assertion of the 'yet' and the 'even so' which, in Biblical Hebrew, is more often than not simply expressed by the letter *waw*—commonly and unthinkingly translated into English as 'and.' Sometimes, indeed, as in the case of the *Kaddish*, the contrast is expressed by sheer juxtaposition—without any connecting word or prefix.

.According to I Kings 8:27–8, Solomon, after he had built the Temple, prayed:

> But will God in very truth dwell on earth?
> Behold, heaven and the heaven of heavens
>   cannot contain You;
> How much less this house that I have built!
> *Yet* have regard unto the prayer of Your servant,
> And to his supplication, O Lord my God,
> To hearken unto the cry and to the prayer
> Which Your servant prays before You this day.

Psalm 8 begins by invoking the majesty of God as revealed in His creation; and, in verses 4 to 6, continues with:

> When I behold Your heavens, the work of Your
>   fingers,
> The moon and the stars that You have set in place,
> What is man that You are mindful of him,
> Mortal man that You take note of him?
> *Yet* You have made him little less than divine,
> And adorned him with glory and majesty.

An early Rabbinic prayer, to which we have already twice referred in these pages, elaborates on the theme of man's utter insignificance, and then goes on to say:[6]

> Man's advantage over the beast is nought,
> For all is vanity.
> *Nevertheless*, we are Your people,
> The partners of Your covenant,
> The sons of Abraham, Your friend . . .

And the well-known *Kaddish* prayer presents a veritable thesaurus of praises of God—in full awareness of man's inability to praise God adequately:[7]

> Blessed and praised,
> Glorified and exalted,
> Extolled and honored,
> Magnified and lauded
> Be the name of the Holy One, praised be He—
> *Although* He transcends all the blessings and hymns,
> Praises and consolations,
> Which can be uttered in the world.

It is, then, in this tradition that the author of the Hymn of the Glory (poem no. 2) can say:

> Your glory I shall tell, though I have never
> seen You.
> I know not what You are, but image can
> describe You.

On a more daring level, Isaac bar Shalom not only declares, 'There is none like You among the dumb' (poem no. 6), but he meant his gruesome description of the destruction of a medieval Jewish community to be inserted in that part of the liturgy where God is celebrated as Israel's Redeemer. The prayerbook proclaims:[8]

> True it is that You are the Lord our God
>   and the God of our fathers,
> Our King, our fathers' King,
> Our Redeemer, our fathers' Redeemer,
> Our Maker, the Rock of our salvation,
> Our Deliverer and our Rescuer,
> Your name is from eternity;
> There is no God beside You.

But just before the prayerbook goes on to say:[9]

> You have been the help of our fathers from of old,
> A Shield and a Savior to their children after them,
> In every single generation,

Isaac bar Shalom cries out, 'There is none like You among the dumb!' and tells his tale of woe.

Something of that kind of contrapuntal effect was attempted in a Conservative prayerbook recently published in the United States. In the *Kaddish*, the doxology *par excellence*, which concludes the martyrology of the Additional Service of the Day of Atonement, each phrase is coupled with the name of a place notorious for the pogroms and for the genocide committed there:[10]

> *Yithgaddal*—Kishinev
> *Veyithqaddash*—Warsaw
> *Shemé rabba*—Auschwitz . . .

Here we have an affirmation of faith which suffering cannot destroy, and, at the same time, a piety profound enough to allow for accusations hurled at God. Isaac bar Shalom no doubt attempted something very similar in the twelfth century.

Such contrapuntal effects and such juxtapositions of opposites all presuppose a considerable intellectual effort on the part of the worshipper. Thought is required as well as devotion, analysis and synthesis in addition to enthusiastic faith.

As long as they were still understood, the *piyyutim* catered to that intellectual component of the Jewish worship experience. The charge often brought against the *piyyutim* in the nineteenth century, that they are difficult to comprehend, and that much biblical and Rabbinic learning was required for their proper understanding, is a charge to which their authors would certainly have pleaded guilty—and with pride. The modern worshipper and even many a modern student may wish to denigrate and to dismiss the *piyyutim* as 'riddles.' But it was Eleazar Kallir, one of the main founders of that art, who joyfully and intentionally *introduced* the *piyyutim* as such. He begins his poetic treatment of the Prayer for Dew on the first day of Passover by saying:[11]

> *beda'to abi'ah ḥidoth*
> *be'am zu bezo betal lehaḥadoth.*
> With His (God's) approval, I shall utter riddles
> To make happy this people [Israel] in this [service]
> with [this prayer for] dew.

Perhaps, unlike his ancestors, the modern Jew goes to his synagogue primarily—if not exclusively—for the purpose of edification. He relegates the aesthetic and intellectual joys of 'problem solving' to the crossword puzzle in his daily newspaper. The medieval synagogue was more comprehensive. It made 'problem solving' and other intellectual 'games' a part of the total worship experience. Many of the *piyyutim* remain as eloquent witnesses of this—products of mind and heart, of thought and of faith.

Notes

Introduction

1 *Jewish Theology*, Assen, 1971, p. 2
2 ibid., p. 1
3 See *Anselm: Fides Quaerens Intellectum*, London, 1960
4 Exodus 33: 18–23
5 *Critique of Religion and Philosophy*, New York, 1958, pp. 163–73
6 ibid., pp. 261ff.
7 *Essays*, Chicago, 1967, p. 62
8 Moses Maimonides, *Guide of the Perplexed*, trs. Shlomo Pines, Chicago, 1963, pp. 137–43
9 Abraham Ibn Ezra, *Commentary on Ecclesiastes* 5:1
10 See Jakob J. Petuchowski, *Prayerbook Reform in Europe*, New York, 1968, pp. 353ff.
11 *The Kingly Crown*, newly trs. with introduction and notes by Bernard Lewis, London, 1961
12 *Die religiöse Gedankenwelt des Salomo Ibn Gabirol*, Leipzig, 1930
13 'The Jewish year,' *Jewish Quarterly Review*, 11 (1899), p. 73
14 See *Ever Since Sinai: A Modern View of Torah*, 2nd ed., New York, 1968; *Heirs of the Pharisees*, New York, 1970

Chapter I The Poetry of the Synagogue

1 For the standard prayers mentioned, without their poetic embellishments, see *The Authorised Daily Prayer Book*, ed. Simeon Singer, 15th ed., London, 1935, pp. 136–8, 128–36, 113a–113d
2 *Sepher Ha'ittim*, ed. Jacob Schorr, Cracow, 1902, p. 252
3 See Michael Avi-Yonah, *In the Days of Rome and Byzantium* (Hebrew), 3rd ed., Jerusalem, 1962, p. 215
4 Martin Schreiner, 'Samau'al b. Jahjâ al-Magrabi und seine Schrift "Ifḥâm

al-Jahûd," ' *Monatsschrift für Geschichte und Wissenschaft des Judentums*, 42 (1898), p. 220

5 Aaron Mirsky, *Reshith Hapiyyut*, Jerusalem, 5725, p. 47

6 ibid., pp. 61ff.

7 A. M. Habermann, *A History of Hebrew Liturgical and Secular Poetry* (Hebrew), vol. 1, Ramat-Gan, 1970, p. 33

8 Ezra Fleischer, 'Piyyut,' in *Encyclopaedia Judaica*, vol. 13, col. 574

9 Habermann, op. cit., p. 36

10 Hayyim (Jefim) Schirmann, 'Appendix about the age of Yannai's life (Hebrew),' *Keshet*, 6 (3), (1964), pp. 64–6

11 Mirsky, op. cit., pp. 86ff.

12 ibid., pp. 11ff.

13 *Mahatzabhtan shel tzuroth hapiyyut*, Jerusalem and Tel-Aviv, 1968

14 'Hebrew liturgical poetry and Christian hymnology,' *Jewish Quarterly Review*, n.s., 44 (1953–4), p. 134

15 *A Social and Religious History of the Jews*, 2nd ed., vol. 7, Philadelphia, 1958, p. 89

16 'Iyyunim bibhe'ayoth taphqidam haliturgi shel sugé hapiyyut haqadum,' *Tarbiz*, 40 (1970), p. 52

17 ibid., p. 60

18 ibid., pp. 55ff.

19 ibid., p. 53

20 See Jakob J. Petuchowski, *Understanding Jewish Prayer*, New York, 1972, pp. 3–16

21 Fleischer, op. cit., pp. 44ff.

22 See Menahem Zulay, *Zur Liturgie der babylonischen Juden*, Stuttgart, 1933, pp. 83ff.

23 See Pirqoi ben Baboi, in *Ginzé Schechter*, ed. Louis Ginzberg, vol. 2, New York, 1929, pp. 504–73

24 See Baron, op. cit., p. 100

25 *Otzar Hageonim*, ed. Benjamin M. Lewin, Haifa, 1928, p. 70

26 See A. A. Wolff, *Die Stimmen der ältesten glaubwürdigsten Rabbinen über die Pijutim*, Leipzig, 1857

27 *Seder Rabh 'Amram Gaon*, ed. E. D. Goldschmidt, Jerusalem, 1971, pp. 167ff., no. 127

28 *Siddur Rabh Saadya Gaon*, ed. Davidson, Assaf and Joel, Jerusalem, 1941, p. 264

29 *Responsa*, ed. J. Blau, Jerusalem, 1960, vol. 2, pp. 467ff.

30 Chicago, 1963, pp. 137–43

31 *Sepher Ḥasidim*, ed. Reuben Margaliot, Jerusalem, 5717, p. 221

32 Jerusalem, 1971, vol. 13, cols 575ff.

Chapter II 'The Creed Should be Sung!'

1 See *The Authorised Daily Prayer Book*, ed. Simeon Singer, 15th ed., London, 1935, pp. 37–44

2 On the early fourteenth-century origin of the poetic version, see Ismar

Elbogen, *Der jüdische Gottesdienst in seiner geschichtlichen Entwicklung*, 4th ed., Hildesheim, 1962, pp. 87–8. On the fifteenth-century date of the prose version, see *Encyclopaedia Judaica*, vol. 3, cols 4–5, *s.v.* Ani Maamin

3 See *Authorised Daily Prayer Book*, pp. 2–3, 122b–122c

4 ibid., pp. 89–90

5 See the discussion and the references to the relevant literature in Louis Jacobs, *Principles of the Jewish Faith*, New York, 1964, pp. 1–32

6 *Targum Pseudo-Jonathan* to Genesis 4:8

7 pal. *Sanhedrin* X, 1, Krotoshin ed., p. 27d

8 See the English translation of this section of Maimonides' Mishnah commentary by J. Abelson in *Jewish Quarterly Review*, 19 (1907), pp. 24–58; and Arthur Hyman, 'Maimonides' "Thirteen Principles,"' in Alexander Altmann, ed., *Jewish Medieval and Renaissance Studies*, Cambridge, Mass., 1967, pp. 119–44

9 Julius Guttmann, *Philosophies of Judaism*, trs. David W. Silverman, Philadelphia, 1964, p. 179

10 See Chaim Bermant, *Troubled Eden*, New York, 1970, pp. 239–53

11 See Aaron Rothkoff, in *Encyclopaedia Judaica*, vol. 16, cols 833–4, *s.v.* Yigdal. Israel Davidson, *Thesaurus*, vol. 4, p. 493, lists ninety-four poetic treatments of the Maimonidean principles

12 See Davidson, *Thesaurus*, vol. 2, pp. 266ff.

13 See *Liberal Jewish Prayer Book*, ed. Israel I. Mattuck, vol. 1, London, 1926, p. 406

14 See A. Z. Idelsohn, *Jewish Music in its Historical Development*, New York, 1929, p. 221

Chapter III Speaking of God

1 Among the whole spate of recent books addressed to that concern, the following deserve to be singled out: Antony Flew and Alasdair MacIntyre, eds, *New Essays in Philosophical Theology*, London, 1955; Antony Flew, *God and Philosophy*, London, 1966; Frederick Ferré, *Language, Logic and God*, New York, 1969; Langdon Gilkey, *Naming the Whirlwind: the Renewal of God-Language*, Indianapolis and New York, 1969

2 b. *'Erubhin* 19a

3 *Tractatus Logico-Philosophicus*, London, 1922, p. 189

4 *Psychoanalysis and Religion*, New Haven, 1950, p. 118

5 b. *Berakhoth* 31b, and frequently in Rabbinic literature

6 *Genesis Rabbah* 19:7

7 See Wilhelm Bacher, *Die exegetische Terminologie der jüdischen Traditionsliteratur*, Leipzig, 1899, part 1, pp. 72ff.

8 Arthur Marmorstein, *The Old Rabbinic Doctrine of God*, vol. 2 (*Essays in Anthropomorphism*), London, 1937

9 *Theology of Ancient Judaism* (Hebrew), 2 vols, London and New York, 1962, 1965

10 *The Immanence of God in Rabbinical Literature*, London, 1912, pp. 151ff.

11 *The Rabbinic Mind*, 2nd ed., New York, 1965, p. 280; and cf. the proofs he

offers for his position throughout that volume. See also his *Organic Thinking*, New York, 1938, Index, *s.v.* Anthropomorphism

12 See James Drummond, *Philo Judaeus*, London and Edinburgh, 1888, vol. 2, pp. 11–15, 41, 245ff.

13 Chicago, 1963, pp. 5ff.

14 See Alexander Altmann, *Studies in Religious Philosophy and Mysticism*, Ithaca, 1969, pp. 152ff.; Joseph Dan, *The Esoteric Theology of Ashkenazi Hasidism* (Hebrew), Jerusalem, 1968, pp. 105ff.

15 See Altmann, op. cit., p. 159

16 See *Encyclopaedia Judaica*, vol. 7, cols 1377–83; Gershom G. Scholem, *Major Trends in Jewish Mysticism*, Jerusalem, 1941, pp. 79–118

17 See Ephraim E. Urbach, in his edition of *Sepher 'Arugath Habosem*, vol. 4, Jerusalem, 1963, pp. 73–111

18 See Dan, op. cit., p. 32

19 ibid., pp. 39ff.

20 See Scholem, op. cit., p. 110; Dan, op. cit., pp. 84ff.

21 See Dan, op. cit., pp. 88ff.

22 *Essays*, Chicago, 1967, p. 42

Chapter IV 'On Account of our Sins'

1 *The Authorised Daily Prayer Book*, ed. Simeon Singer, 15th ed., London, 1935, p. 234

2 Ed. E. D. Goldschmidt, Jerusalem, 1971, p. 153. We have expressed ourselves somewhat cautiously about the inclusion of the poem in that work, since there is an element of doubt in connection with any actual *texts*, as contrasted with the liturgical instructions, contained in the various editions of 'Amram's prayerbook which are in circulation

3 *Die synagogale Poesie des Mittelalters*, Berlin, 1855

4 This chapter has been published separately in an English translation entitled *The Sufferings of the Jews during the Middle Ages*, New York, 1907

5 For details of the various Reform liturgies mentioned, and for the actual Hebrew texts, see Jakob J. Petuchowski, *Prayerbook Reform in Europe*, New York, 1968, pp. 252–64

6 H. N. Bialik, *Kol Kithbhé Ḥayyim Naḥman Bialik*, Tel-Aviv, 1938, p. 84

7 *God's Presence in History*, New York, 1970, p. 73

8 *Faith after the Holocaust*, New York, 1973, p. 94

9 In Donald R. Cutler, ed., *The Religious Situation: 1968*, Boston, 1968, p. 61; cf. his *After Auschwitz*, Indianapolis, 1966, *passim*

Chapter V 'Measure for Measure'

1 *The Religious Imagination*, Indianapolis, 1968, p. 127

2 ibid., p. 135

3 See Leopold Zunz, *Literaturgeschichte der synagogalen Poesie*, Berlin, 1865, pp. 111–15, 235–8; A. M. Habermann, ed., *Liturgical Poems of R. Shim'on bar Yiṣḥaq* (Hebrew), Berlin, 1938, pp. 7–18

4 Jeremiah 12:1. For this translation see Sheldon H. Blank, *Jeremiah, Man and Prophet*, Cincinnati, 1961, p. 111
5 See Nahum N. Glatzer, ed., *In Time and Eternity*, New York, 1946, pp. 94ff.
6 See *Mishnah Sotah* 1:7–9; b. *Megillah* 12b; and cf. Ephraim E. Urbach, *The Sages: their Concepts and Beliefs* (Hebrew), Jerusalem, 1969, pp. 384–7, 404–5

Chapter VI Tamar's Pledge

1 See Arthur Davis and Herbert M. Adler, eds, *Service of the Synagogue*, Passover volume, 13th ed., London, 1949, pp. 218, 228ff.
2 E.g., Hosea, chapters 1 and 2
3 E.g., Jeremiah 2:2
4 *Authorised Daily Prayer Book*, ed. Simeon Singer, 15th ed., London, 1935, pp. 7ff.; cf. b. *Yoma* 87b

Chapter VII The Silent God

1 See *Authorised Daily Prayer Book*, ed. Simeon Singer, 15th ed., London, 1935, p. 44
2 b. *Yoma* 69b; and see Jakob J. Petuchowski, *Understanding Jewish Prayer*, New York, 1972, pp. 64ff.
3 b. *Yoma* 69b
4 ibid.
5 b. *Gittin* 56b
6 ibid.
7 See the discussion by Samuel Edels (*Maharsha*) in his commentary ad loc.

Chapter VIII The Suffering God

1 *Exodus Rabbah* 2:5
2 *Mekhilta, Masekheth dePisha*, chapter 14, ed. Horovitz-Rabin, p. 51; and cf. *Siphré, Beha'alothekha*, pisqa 84, ed. Friedmann, p. 22b
3 *Exodus Rabbah*, loc. cit.; *Mekhilta*, loc. cit.; *Siphré*, loc. cit.
4 *Lamentations Rabbah*, petihta 34, ed. Buber, p. 19b, and *Pesiqta deRabh Kahana*, pisqa 13, ed. Buber, p. 113b
5 *Lamentations Rabbah*, loc. cit., and *Pesiqta deRabh Kahana*, loc. cit. This interpretation of Ezekiel 1:1 is based on the assumption that *ani* ('I') is a divine name. See Jacob Levy, *Wörterbuch über die Talmudim und Midraschim*, 2nd ed., Berlin, 1924, vol. 1, p. 110, *s.v. Ani*
6 *Tanhuma, Tetzé*, paragraph 18, ed. Buber, p. 23a; cf. Rashi to Exodus 17:16
7 Genesis 36:12
8 Cf. Gershom G. Scholem, *Major Trends in Jewish Mysticism*, Jerusalem, 1941, pp. 270ff.
9 *Mekhilta*, loc. cit.; cf. *Siphré*, loc. cit., and *Yalqut Shime'oni*, II Samuel, no. 146

10 *Essays*, Chicago, 1967, pp. 11–84. This particular essay first appeared in the *Hebrew Union College Annual*, vol. 27 (1956)
11 ibid., p. 48
12 ibid.
13 ibid., p. 56
14 See, e.g., Edgar S. Brightman, *A Philosophy of Religion*, New York, 1940
15 op. cit., p. 48
16 *Some Aspects of Rabbinic Theology*, London, 1909, p. 46
17 ibid., p. 12

Chapter IX A Somber View of Man

1 *Psychoanalysis and Religion*, New Haven, 1959, p. 35
2 *Israelitisches Gebetbuch*, ed. Abraham Geiger, Berlin, 1870, vol. 2, pp. 245ff.
3 *Gebetbuch für das ganze Jahr*, ed. C. Seligmann, I. Elbogen, and H. Vogelstein, Frankfurt aM, 1929, vol. 2, pp. 330–2
4 *Union Prayer Book*, newly revised, vol. 2, Cincinnati, 1945, pp. 210ff.
5 op. cit., p. 37 (italics in the original).
6 *Tanhuma, Tazri'a* 7, ed. Buber, p. 18
7 *Genesis Rabbah* 9:12
8 *Tanḥuma, Beshallaḥ*, 14, ed. Buber, p. 31a
9 *Mekhilta, Yithro*, par. 2, ed. Horovitz-Rabın, p. 196; *Mekhilta deRabbi Shime'on b. Yohai, Yithro*, ed. Epstein-Melamed, p. 132; b. *Shabbath* 10a; *Midrash leqaḥ Tobh, Yithro* 10, ed. Buber, p. 62a
10 b. *Shabbath* 119b
11 For a collection of relevant source materials, see Michael Guttmann, *Clavis Talmudis*, vol. 1, part 1, Budapest, 1910, pp. 514–621; H. N. Bialik and J. H. Rawnitzky, eds, *Sepher Ha-Aggadah*, 3rd ed., Tel-Aviv, 1960, pp. 451–538. For modern treatments of that material, see George Foot Moore, *Judaism*, Cambridge, Mass., 1927, vol. 1, pp. 445–552; A. Cohen, *Everyman's Talmud*, London, 1949, pp. 67–120; Ephraim E. Urbach, *The Sages: their Concepts and Beliefs* (Hebrew), Jerusalem, 1969, pp. 190–226
12 b. *'Erubhin* 13b
13 *Aus drei Jahrtausenden*, 2nd ed., Tübingen, 1958, p. 24
14 op. cit., pp. 224–6
15 Cf. b. *Yoma* 87b
16 *The Authorised Daily Prayer Book*, ed. Simeon Singer, 15th ed., London, 1935, pp. 7ff., and cf. *Seder Rabh 'Amram Gaon*, ed. E. D. Goldschmidt, Jerusalem, 1971, p. 6
17 H. Brody and M. Wiener, eds, *Anthologia Hebraica*, Leipzig, 1922, p. 88, and Israel Davidson, ed., *Selected Religious Poems of Solomon Ibn Gabirol*, Philadelphia, 1923, p. 61
18 See Frederick P. Bargebuhr, *The Alhambra*, Berlin, 1968, pp. 49–80
19 *Mishnah Aboth* 4:4
20 ibid., 4:22
21 See in recent years, *High Holiday Prayer Book*, ed. Morris Silverman,

Hartford, 1951, p. 275; and Louis Barish, *High Holiday Liturgy*, New York, 1959, p. 127

22 See Zunz, *Literaturgeschichte der synagogalen Poesie*, Berlin, 1865, p. 109; Landshuth, *'Ammudé Ha'abhodah*, Berlin, 1857–62, p. 268

23 *Mabho Lemaḥzor Bené Roma*, 2nd ed. with notes by E. D. Goldschmidt, Tel-Aviv, 1966, p. 62. In his note ad loc., Goldschmidt states it as a certainty that the poem antedates Meshullam, and he even considers the *possibility* that it might antedate Kallir! The first edition of Luzzatto's work was published in Leghorn in 1856

24 Martin Buber, *Tales of the Hasidim: the Later Masters*, New York, 1948, pp. 249ff.

Chapter X The All-Inclusive Torah

1 Cf. Exodus 3:1ff.; Ezekiel 11:24; Hosea 12:11; and frequently in the Bible
2 Cf. Deuteronomy 5:5; and frequently
3 Cf. Isaiah 2:3, and throughout the Bible. See also Jakob J. Petuchowski, *Ever Since Sinai: a Modern View of Torah*, 2nd ed., New York, 1968, pp. 4–12
4 See Kaufmann Kohler, *Jewish Theology*, New York, 1918, p. 34
5 b. *Gittin* 60b
6 *Mishnah Aboth* 1:1
7 b. *Gittin* 60a
8 Cf. b. *Shabbath* 23a; and see Jakob J. Petuchowski, *Heirs of the Pharisees*, New York, 1970, pp. 61–4
9 See Max Kadushin, *The Rabbinic Mind*, 2nd ed., New York, 1965, pp. 57ff.
10 See Jakob J. Petuchowski, 'The supposed dogma of the Mosaic authorship of the Pentateuch,' *Hibbert Journal*, 57 (1959), pp. 356–60
11 See Julian Morgenstern, 'The oldest document of the Hexateuch,' *Hebrew Union College Annual*, vol. 4 (1927), pp. 1–138; see particularly p. 95
12 See *The Authorised Daily Prayer Book*, ed. Simeon Singer, 15th ed., London, 1935, p. 228
13 See Louis Ginzberg, *The Legends of the Jews*, vol. 3, Philadelphia, 1911, pp. 109–14
14 b. *Sukkah* 5a
15 *Shir Hashirim Rabbah* 6, 3
16 See the Epistle of Barnabas, in James A. Kleist, ed., *Ancient Christian Writers*, vol. 6, London, 1948, pp. 57ff.

Chapter XI Waiting for 'the End'

1 b. *Shabbath* 31a
2 Cf. Isaiah 2:1–5
3 b. *Sanhedrin* 98a
4 ibid. 97b
5 ibid. 98a

6 See Joseph H. Hertz, ed., *The Pentateuch and Haftorahs*, 2nd ed., London, 1960, pp. 710–13; 725–9; 750–4

7 ibid., pp. 776–9; 794–8; 818–19; 835–9; 857–8; 874–7; 883–6

Epilogue

1 4 vols, 2nd ed., New York, 1970

2 *Prayerbook for Pesach*, arr. Wolf Heidenheim, English trs. Jenny Marmorstein, Victor Goldschmidt, Basle, 1967, pp. 1–100

3 *The Book of Prayer and Order of Service according to the Custom of the Spanish and Portuguese Jews*, ed. Moses Gaster, vol. 5, London, 1906, pp. 44–110

4 See David Philipson, *The Reform Movement in Judaism*, 3rd ed., New York, 1967, pp. 423ff.

5 See Arthur Davis and Herbert M. Adler, eds, *Service of the Synagogue*, Tabernacles volume, 14th ed., London, 1949, p. vi

6 *The Authorised Daily Prayer Book*, ed. Simeon Singer, 15th ed., London, 1935, p. 8

7 ibid., p. 77

8 ibid., p. 135

9 ibid.

10 *Maḥzor for Rosh Hashanah and Yom Kippur*, ed. Jules Harlow, Rabbinical Assembly, New York, 1972, p. 566

11 *Daily Prayer Book*, ed. Philip Birnbaum, New York, 1949, p. 633; and cf. Jakob J. Petuchowski, *Understanding Jewish Prayer*, New York, 1972, pp. 26ff.

Index

Printed and bound by CPI Group (UK) Ltd, Croydon, CR0 4YY

09/06/2025

14685793-0001